# WINDOWS 3.1 & WINDOWS® 95

## FOR BEGINNERS

**WINDOWS 3.1 FOR BEGINNERS**

page 1

**PROJECTS FOR WINDOWS 3.1 FOR BEGINNERS**

page 47

**WINDOWS 95 FOR BEGINNERS**

Page 93

# WINDOWS® 3.1 FOR BEGINNERS

## Richard Dungworth
### Edited by Philippa Wingate
Editorial consultants: Jane Chisholm & Anthony Marks

### Designed by Neil Francis & Steve Page
Additional designs by Sarah Bealham, Non Figg & Russell Punter
### Illustrated by Colin Mier, Derek Matthews, Andy Burton, Pete Taylor and Paul Southcombe
Technical Consultant: Richard Payne

# Contents

3 INTRODUCING WINDOWS 3.1
4 DOS, WINDOWS AND APPLICATIONS
6 STARTING AND STOPPING
8 THE WINDOWS 3.1 DESKTOP
10 USING YOUR MOUSE
12 CONTROLLING A WINDOW
14 PROGRAM MANAGER
16 WORD PROCESSING WITH WRITE
18 MORE ABOUT WRITE
20 USING DIALOG BOXES
22 SAVING YOUR WORK
24 MORE ABOUT FILES
26 PAINTBRUSH
28 MORE ABOUT PAINTBRUSH
30 USING FILE MANAGER
32 FINDING YOUR FILES
34 ORGANIZING YOUR FILES
36 PRINTING A DOCUMENT
37 EXPLORING APPLICATIONS
38 WINDOWS 3.1 GADGETS
40 ORGANIZING YOUR DESKTOP
42 COMBINING APPLICATIONS
44 HOW TO GET HELP
46 WINDOWS 3.1 WORDS

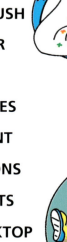

# Introducing Windows 3.1

You can use your personal computer, or PC, for all sorts of amazing jobs. But before it can perform even the simplest task, your PC needs a list of instructions, called a program. To make sure that your computer has all the instructions it needs, you can buy whole sets of programs, grouped together as software.

*Your computer needs software before it can work.*

## What is Microsoft Windows?

Microsoft® Windows® is a special piece of software which enables you to tell your PC what you want it to do. You use Windows to control all the other software on your computer. This section of the book explains the simple techniques you'll need to become one of the 80 million people who use Windows to control their PC.

*Windows lets you control your PC quickly and easily.*

## Windows versions

From time to time Microsoft brings out a new version of the Windows system. The new version includes various improvements on earlier versions. Each Windows version is given a number. The higher the number, the more recent is the version.

This section of the book concentrates on version 3.1 of the Windows software. Its screen pictures show the Windows® 3.1 display. But you can use the same techniques to operate other versions of Windows, including Windows® 3.11.

## Windows 95

The most advanced version of Microsoft Windows is called Windows® 95. You can find out about it in the third section of this book, which starts on page 93.

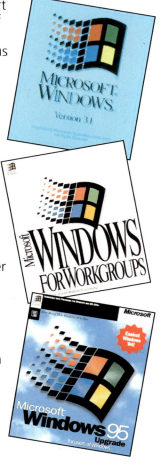

## About this section

This section of the book introduces all the main features of Windows 3.1, telling you how to use them step-by-step. The first time you read it, work through it page by page from beginning to end. Later, you can use the index at the back of the book to look up particular topics to refresh your memory.

## Getting help

Some pages include "help" boxes with a lifebelt in the top left-hand corner. These boxes contain tips to help you cope as you find your way around Windows.

If you need extra help, you can find out on pages 44 and 45 how to use the instructions that are included in the Windows 3.1 software.

# DOS, Windows and applications

In order to work properly, a computer needs a piece of software called an operating system. One of an operating system's main jobs is to take in commands from the person using the computer (known as the user) and convert them into instructions which the computer can understand.

## How does Windows work?

The Windows system fills your PC's display with pictures. By "touching" or moving these pictures in a particular way, using an on-screen pointer, you can tell Windows what you want your computer to do. Windows then controls DOS on your behalf to make your computer carry out your commands.

*This screen shows the Windows 3.1 display.*

You will find out about the different pictures which make up the Windows 3.1 display on pages 8 and 9.

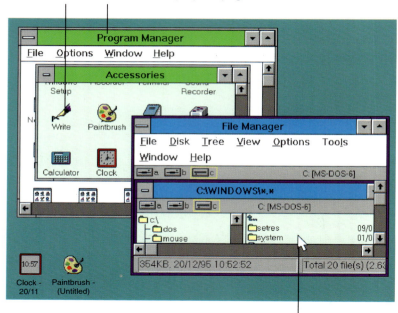

## MS-DOS

Most personal computers use an operating system called Microsoft Disk Operating System. It is known as MS-DOS or DOS for short. With DOS, you tell your computer what to do by typing in command codes using your PC's keyboard. Some DOS commands are rather complicated.

To make DOS easier to use, Microsoft developed the Windows system. Windows works with DOS to enable you to control your computer without having to type in DOS commands.

**This pointer enables you to touch specific parts of the display.**

## Mouse control

Instead of using your computer's keyboard to control the Windows pointer, you move it around using a hand-held device, connected to the computer by a thin cable. Because of its shape and its cable "tail", this gadget is known as a mouse.

You will find out how to use your computer's mouse on pages 10 and 11 of this book.

4

## Application software

Windows enables your PC to use, or "run", other pieces of software, called applications. Each application includes the instructions and information that your computer needs to play a particular role.

You can buy applications for a remarkable range of jobs. Games, drawing programs, and so-called spreadsheets and databases are all examples of applications. The picture below shows some of the things you can do with your PC by running applications.

## Compatibility

When you buy an application to use with Windows on your PC, you must make sure that it is designed to be controlled with Windows, rather than with another operating system. Applications which work with the Windows system are said to be Windows compatible.

## What you need to begin

To use Windows 3.1, you need a PC which can run the Windows 3.1 software. Windows 3.1 and its applications were designed for use on computers built by a company called IBM. But other companies now sell PCs which are "IBM compatible" and can use the Windows system.

*Some computers which run Windows 3.1 are small enough to fit on your lap.*

## Installing Windows 3.1

Most PCs already have DOS and Windows 3.1 software when you buy them. If yours doesn't, you need to buy the software and feed it into your PC. This is known as installing the software. Follow the installation instructions that are included with the software.

## Standard applications

The applications used in this book to introduce Windows 3.1 techniques are included in the Windows 3.1 software when you buy it. So you don't need to buy any extra software to start learning.

*You will find out on pages 16-21 how to use an application called Write to create a letter to a friend.*

*Pages 26-29 explain how you can use the Paintbrush application to draw pictures.*

# Starting and stopping

Before you can use Windows 3.1, you need to switch on your computer, and start the Windows software running.

## Switching on

To switch on your computer, press its power switch. You also need to switch on the piece of equipment that shows your PC's display, called a monitor. Some monitors automatically come on when the computer that they're connected to is switched on, but others have a separate on/off switch.

Your computer will begin to make whirring noises. Long lists of command codes will begin to scroll up your screen. If this doesn't happen, check that all the power leads are plugged in properly, and that the electricity is switched on at the socket.

### WARNING!
Electricity from the mains socket can be very dangerous. Never fiddle with plugs when the mains switch is on.

## Running Windows 3.1

Once your computer is switched on, you need to make sure the Windows 3.1 software is running. Most computers which use Windows either automatically run the Windows 3.1 software, or start up in DOS (see page 4).

If your PC is set to run the Windows software automatically, your screen will briefly show a picture of a multicoloured flag (the Windows logo) before filling with the Windows 3.1 display.

If your computer starts in DOS, the "DOS prompt", shown below, will appear on your screen.

**The DOS prompt**

In this case you need to start Windows 3.1 running yourself. Type the letters WIN and press the **Return** key. The Windows logo and display will then appear on your screen.

## Keystroke commands

As you work through this book, you will occasionally need to use your computer's keyboard to enter a command. This is known as using keystrokes. The keystrokes included in this book are printed in bold type, **like this**. Although keyboards vary, the diagram below should help you find the keys you need.

*This diagram shows the typical layout of a PC's keyboard.*

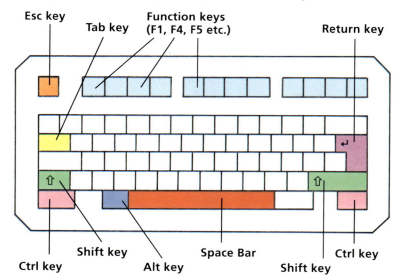

6

## Computer health

Once you have successfully started Windows 3.1 running, you can find out how to use it by working through the rest of this book. However, long periods of computing may damage your health. So, as you work with your PC, it is important to take a break at least once an hour. When you take a short break, you can leave your computer switched on.

## Screen savers

Don't be alarmed if you return after a break to find an unusual screen display. A monitor's screen can be damaged by showing the same image for a long time. So Windows often puts a moving "screen saver" on display if your mouse and keyboard are left untouched for a while.

The Windows display will return as soon as you give your mouse a nudge.

*This screen shows an example of a Windows screen saver.*

### HELP!

When you disturb a screen saver, a box like the one below may appear on your screen. This means that the screen saver is "locked" on. To return to the Windows 3.1 display you will need to ask the person who set this lock for their screen saver password.

## Shutting down

Another important thing to know is how to stop when you've finished using Windows 3.1 for the day. This is known as shutting down.

Before you switch off your PC's power supply, you must bring your Windows 3.1 session to an end. Switching off the power while Windows is still running can damage your computer.

## Ending your session

When you are ready to shut down, follow the steps below to bring your Windows 3.1 session to an end:

1 - Make sure that you have selected the part of the Windows 3.1 system called Program Manager. You will find out how to do this on page 9.

2 - While holding down the **Alt** key, press the **F4** key. Release both keys.

3 - The box shown below will appear on your screen. If you have changed your mind about stopping, press and release the **Esc** key. Otherwise press and release the **Return** key.

As Windows 3.1 stops running, its display will vanish from the screen, and your computer will return to DOS. Once the DOS prompt appears, you can safely switch off your PC and monitor.

# The Windows 3.1 desktop

Once Windows is running, it fills your screen with a display called the desktop. Your desktop may be almost empty to begin with, but as you work with Windows, it will become crowded with pictures, like the example shown on the right. These pages introduce the main parts of the Windows 3.1 desktop.

*This screen shows a crowded Windows 3.1 desktop.*

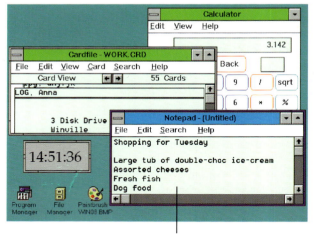

## Programs and pictures

Just like an ordinary desk, a busy Windows 3.1 desktop is scattered with useful items. But instead of providing a real notepad, calculator, address book, or clock, Windows spreads out programs that do the same jobs as these articles. Each picture on the desktop represents one of these programs. There are two main types of desktop picture, called windows and icons.

When an item on the Windows 3.1 desktop overlaps others, it is described as being nearer the top of the desktop.

## What is a window?

A window is a rectangular box, with a thin border on all four sides, and a thicker strip across its top edge. The picture below shows what a typical window looks like, and what its various parts are called. You will find out on pages 12 and 13 what a window's borders, buttons and bars are for.

*A window*

This small square with a slot in is called a control-menu box.

This strip across the top edge of a window is called a title bar.

Most windows have a second strip containing a row of words. This is called a menu bar.

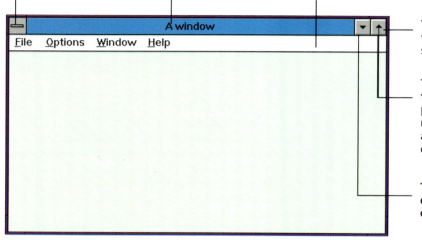

The top right-hand corner of each window contains two small squares which look like buttons.

This button can appear in two forms. If it shows a single upward pointing arrow it is called a maximize button. But if it shows a double-arrow like this, it is called a restore button.

This button, showing a downward pointing arrow, is called a minimize button.

8

## Icons

Instead of appearing as a window, a program can be represented on the desktop by a small picture, called an icon. Icons can appear anywhere on your desktop. They are often found along the bottom edge of your screen.

An icon usually has a label underneath it, giving the name of the program it represents.

*These are some of the icons that you will come across on your Windows desktop.*

File Manager    Paintbrush    Clock    Calculator

Write    Notepad    Cardfile    Calendar

The appearance of a program's icon often provides a clue to what that program is for. For example, the icon for Paintbrush, a program which lets you draw pictures, looks like an artist's paint palette and brush.

## The pointer

Somewhere on your desktop you'll find the pointer (see page 4). The pointer usually appears as a small arrowhead, but depending on what you are using it for, it can take on any of the forms shown below.

*The arrowhead pointer*     *Other pointer shapes*

## Wallpaper

The Windows 3.1 desktop is sometimes decorated with a patterned layer, called wallpaper. There are lots of different designs.

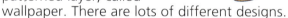

*This screen shows an example of Windows wallpaper.*

## Finding Program Manager

On the next two pages of this book you'll find out how to use your mouse to control the Windows 3.1 desktop. You'll use a window called Program Manager for this mouse practice, so you need to make sure that the Program Manager window is on top of your desktop.

Hold down the **Alt** key. When you press and release the **Tab** key, a box containing an icon and its name will appear in the middle of your screen. If the icon and name are different from those shown in the box below, keep the **Alt** key held down and press and release the **Tab** key again. Keep doing this until the box shows Program Manager's icon and name as shown below.

Now release the **Alt** key and Program Manager's window will jump to the top of your desktop. To make sure the window fills your screen, hold down the **Alt** key and press the **Space Bar**. Release both keys, and type the letter **X**.

You'll find out more about Program Manager on pages 14 and 15.

# Using your mouse

Now that you know what the Windows 3.1 desktop looks like, you can find out how to use it to tell your computer what to do.

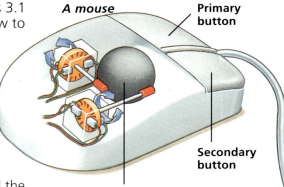

*A mouse* — **Primary button**, **Secondary button**

As you move the mouse, the motion of this ball is converted into movement of the pointer across your screen.

## Pointing things out

To operate the desktop, you use the on-screen pointer as an electronic finger to pick out and move around specific parts of the display. You control the pointer's movements using a mouse (see page 4). The picture on the right shows a computer mouse, cut away so that you can see inside.

Most mice have two switches on their top surface, called the primary and secondary mouse buttons. The primary button is usually on the left, as shown in the picture. But if your computer is set for a left-handed mouse user, the buttons swap positions.

## Mouse movements

Try moving your mouse about on a flat, clean surface. The pointer will follow your mouse movements by moving across the screen.

*This is how you hold your mouse.*

Use a special mouse mat if you have one, but a hardback book or a clear area of desk will do.

## Clicking

To "touch" part of the display, use your mouse to move the pointer over it, and then press and release the primary mouse button (see above). This is called clicking. It is the main way in which you use your mouse to control Windows.

You can click on various bits of the desktop, some of which look like buttons. Have a go at clicking on the restore button in the top right-hand corner of Program Manager's window on your screen (see page 8). Clicking on this button will cause the window to shrink so that it covers only part of the desktop, rather than filling the whole screen.

*Clicking*

1. Press the primary mouse button.

2. Release the button.

If your mouse reaches the edge of the surface that you're using it on, lift it up and replace it near the middle of the surface. By lifting your mouse, you can reposition it on your work surface without altering the position of the pointer on your screen. Use this technique to make the space you need to move your mouse in the direction you want.

10

## Dragging

To move something around on the desktop, you use another mouse technique, called dragging.

Position the pointer over the item you want to move. Press and hold down the primary mouse button. Imagine that you are grabbing and holding on to the item. By keeping the primary button depressed as you move your mouse, you can drag the item to another area of the desktop. Once it is where you want it, release the mouse button to drop the item into its new desktop location.

Try out your dragging technique by moving the Program Manager window to a new position on your desktop. To move the window, drag its title bar.

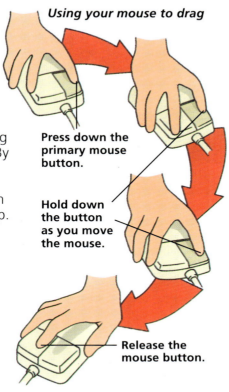

*Using your mouse to drag*

**Press down the primary mouse button.**

**Hold down the button as you move the mouse.**

**Release the mouse button.**

## Mouse lessons

To improve your mouse skills, you can use a lesson which is included in the Windows 3.1 software. This is how you start the lesson:

1 - Make sure that the Program Manager window is selected (see page 9).

2 - While holding down the **Alt** key, type the letter **H**. Release both keys.

3 - Type the letter **W**.

Now follow the instructions which appear on your screen to use the Mouse Lesson. When you have had enough mouse practice, press the **Esc** key to return to the desktop display.

## Double-clicking

The final mouse technique is called double-clicking. This is a special way of touching an item on the desktop. To double-click on part of your display, move the pointer over it and press and release the primary mouse button twice in quick succession.

Double-clicking usually offers a shortcut way to do something. For example, double-clicking on a window's title bar provides a speedy way to change the window's size. Try out your double-click on the Program Manager window's title bar.

'Click' 'Click'

### HELP!

If you lose sight of Program Manager as you try out your mouse skills, you can bring it back to the top of your desktop using the **Alt** and **Tab** keys (see page 9). You'll find out more about how to find things on your Windows desktop on pages 40 & 41.

# Controlling a window

A window provides a workspace on your desktop in which you can use a particular program. Now that you can click, drag and double-click, you need to know how to use these mouse skills to control a typical window, so that you can work with Windows programs.

## Open windows

Windows that appear on your desktop are said to be open. Your computer can run several programs at the same time, so several windows can be open on the desktop. However, you can only use one of these open windows at a time.

## Active or inactive?

When a particular window is in use it is known as the active window. It lies on top of the other "inactive" windows on your desktop, and usually has a different coloured title bar.

When you want to use a specific window, you can make it active by clicking on any part of it. If you can't do this because the window is hidden by other items on your desktop, you will need to use one of the techniques described on pages 40 and 41 to "switch" to the window that you want to use.

*A busy desktop*

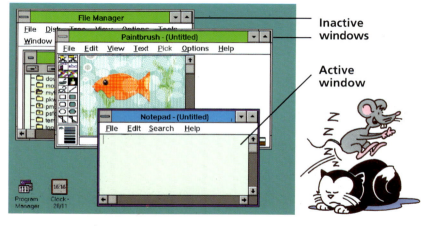

## Minimizing

If your desktop gets crowded with open windows, you can make some space by reducing the amount of room taken up by windows that you're not currently working with. By clicking on the minimize button in the top right-hand corner of a window, you can reduce that window to an icon at the bottom of your screen. This is known as minimizing a window.

Minimizing lets you put a program to one side for the time being. If you want to use that program again, you can convert its icon back into a window by double-clicking on it. Returning a window to its original size and location on your desktop is known as restoring that window.

*Minimizing and restoring*

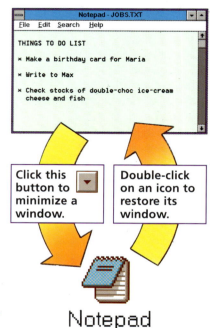

# Maximizing

If you want more space inside a particular window, you can expand it so that it fills your screen. To do this, click on the window's maximize button.

A window which has been maximized fills the entire screen and has no surrounding border. Instead of a maximize button it has a restore button. You can return the window to its previous size and position by clicking this restore button.

*Maximizing and restoring*

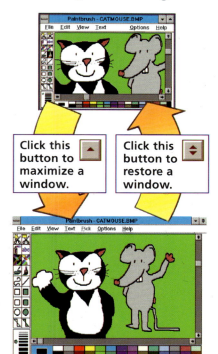

# Changing a window's size

You can adjust the size of a window, stretching or shrinking it to make it wider, narrower, taller or shorter. To alter a window's size, point to the border that you want to move. The pointer will change into a double-headed arrow, showing the directions in which you can alter the window's shape. Hold down the mouse button and drag the border to a new position.

*This diagram shows you the different ways in which you can change a window's size.*

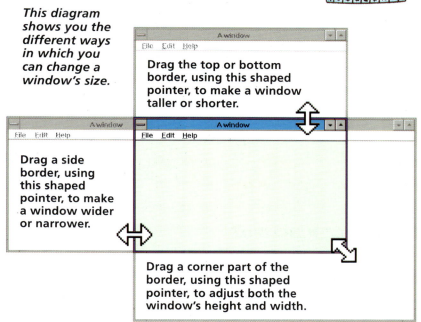

# Using scroll bars

Sometimes a window isn't big enough to display all its contents. When this is the case, the window has a "scroll bar" along its right edge, its bottom edge, or both these edges. You can use these scroll bars to shift the window's view so that you can look at any part of its contents.

To move your view a little at a time, click on the arrow button at either end of a scroll bar. To shift your view by a whole window size, click on the scroll bar itself. Or you can drag the small square called the scroll box along the scroll bar until the window shows the area you want.

*A window with scroll bars*

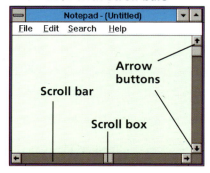

# Moving a window

Unless it has been maximized to fill the screen, you can move a window around the desktop by dragging its title bar to a new location.

13

# Program Manager

To use a Windows program, you need to open its window on your desktop by running that program.
These pages introduce Program Manager, the part of the Windows 3.1 system that lets you find and run the programs that you need. To explore Program Manager, make sure that its window is active and maximized (see pages 12 and 13).

## Program group windows

To find out which programs a particular program group contains, double-click on its program group icon. A window will appear inside the Program Manager window. This type of window is called a program group window. Once a program group window is open, it displays an icon for each of the programs included in that group.

*This screen shows the Accessories program group window open inside Program Manager's window.*

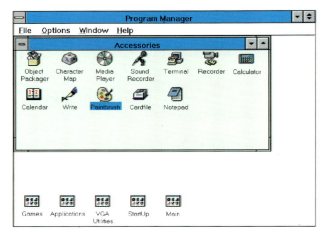

## Tidying the display

When you use the Program Manager window for the first time, it's a good idea to tidy up your display, so that you can see where everything is. To do this, hold down the **Shift** key, and press the **F5** key. If any open windows appear inside the Program Manager window, minimize them one by one until your display looks like this:

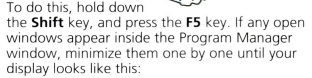

**Several icons will line up along the bottom of the Program Manager window.**

## Program group icons

Program Manager gathers all the programs on your computer into "program groups". Each program group has its own name, and is represented by a "program group icon" inside the Program Manager window.

**Each icon is labelled with the name of the group it represents.**

*A program group icon*

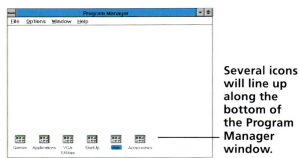

## Finding a program

To run a program that you want to use, you need to find the icon that represents that program. To do this, use Program Manager to open and search each program group window until you find the icon you need. You may have to use scroll bars on a program group window to search its contents thoroughly.

Each time you open a program group window, use the **Shift** and **F5** keys to tidy up the Program Manager window. If Program Manager becomes cluttered with open program group windows, make some space by minimizing the ones you are not using. This will change them back into program group icons.

# Running a program

Once you have found the icon for the program you want, you can start the program running. To do this, you simply double-click on the program's icon.

As a program starts running, its window appears on top of your desktop. The program will remain on your desktop, as a window or an icon, until you stop it running. On page 25 you'll find out how to stop a program running by "closing" its window.

# The way out

The Program Manager window also enables you to bring your Windows 3.1 session to an end. You found out on page 7 how to stop Windows 3.1 running using keystrokes to close the Program Manager window.

Once you've learned how to use clicking to close a window (see page 25) you'll be able to use your mouse, rather than the keyboard, to close Program Manager and quit Windows.

# Using menu commands

Like most other windows, the Program Manager window has a menu bar containing several words. When you click on one of the words in a window's menu bar, a list of possible commands called a menu drops down beneath that word. You can select one of these commands by clicking on it.

Some menus include shortcut keystrokes for certain commands. You can use these as an alternative to using your mouse to enter the command.

Choosing commands from menus is one of the main ways in which you use Windows to control your PC.

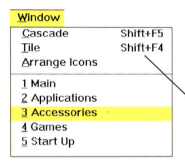

*Try using Program Manager's Window menu, shown here, to open a particular program group window.*

**This keyboard short cut means "hold down the Shift key and press the F4 key".**

# Disabled menu commands

Some of the commands included in a menu may appear in faded text. These are known as disabled commands. Clicking on a disabled menu command has no effect.

Other parts of the Windows 3.1 display, such as command buttons, can also appear in disabled form.

*This menu includes two disabled commands.*

*Disabled buttons like these won't respond to clicking.*

# Word processing with Write

Now that you know how to find and run a program, you can try out a Windows application. Use Program Manager to find the icon for a program called Write. It looks like this, and is usually found in the Accessories program group. Double-click on the Write icon to set the Write application running.

## What is Write?

Write is an application which enables you to work with text. Text is made up of individual units called characters, which can be letters of the alphabet, numbers, punctuation marks, symbols or even spaces. Write lets you type text into your computer and then organize it to form a document such as a letter or story. This kind of application is called a word processing program.

## The Write window

As you start Write running, its window appears on your desktop. This window provides all the tools you will need to create a text document. The area inside the window displays your Write document, which starts off as a blank page. Maximize the Write window to take a closer look at its various parts.

*This screen shows the Write window in maximized form. The top left-hand corner is magnified so that you can see it more clearly.*

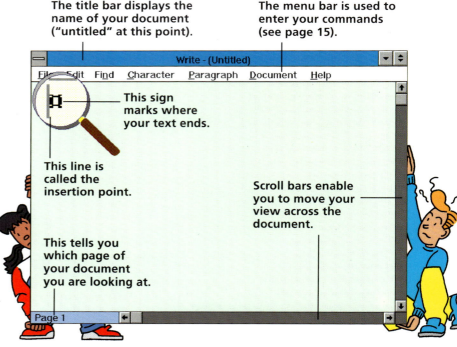

The title bar displays the name of your document ("untitled" at this point).

The menu bar is used to enter your commands (see page 15).

This sign marks where your text ends.

This line is called the insertion point.

Scroll bars enable you to move your view across the document.

This tells you which page of your document you are looking at.

## Entering text

The flashing vertical line inside Write's page area is called the insertion point. It shows you where your text will be placed on the page when you start typing. Try it out by typing in the words "Word processing with Write". As you type, the text will appear to the left of the insertion point, as shown below.

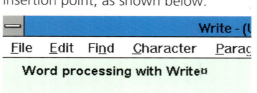

16

## The I-beam

When you point inside Write's page area, the pointer turns into a tall "I" shape. This special pointer is called the I-beam. You use it to position the insertion point anywhere within your document.

Using your mouse, move the I-beam to the left of the word "with". Click the primary mouse button, and the insertion point will jump to this new location. Now type the words "is easy". This new text will insert itself in your document to the left of the insertion point's new position.

## Deleting text

To rub out, or "delete", some of your text, use the I-beam to place the insertion point to the right of the text you want to remove. Press the **Backspace** key to delete one character at a time. The **Backspace** key usually has an arrow on it, pointing to the left. On most keyboards it is found above the **Return** key (see page 6).

Try deleting the words "with Write" that you typed onto your Write page earlier.

*The Backspace key*

## Selecting text

You can also use the I-beam to mark out parts of your document that you want to alter. This is called selecting. To select a section of text, move the I-beam to the left of the first character in that section. Holding down the mouse button, drag the I-beam until it is just to the right of the last character in the section. When you release the mouse button, the selected text remains highlighted, as shown below.

Highlighted Write text looks like this

## Deleting a block

You can delete a chunk of text, known as a text "block", by selecting it and pressing the **Backspace** key. All the highlighted text will be removed from your document. Try deleting the remaining words on your Write page in this way.

## Shortcut selecting

There are several speedy ways to select parts of your document. To select an individual word, simply double-click the I-beam on it. To select an entire line of text, click in the left-hand margin next to that line with the arrow-shaped pointer, or hold down the **Ctrl** key and click the I-beam somewhere along the line. To select your entire document, hold down the **Ctrl** key and click in the left-hand margin with the arrow-shaped pointer.

### WARNING!

While a block of text is selected, any new text that you type in will replace it. To avoid this happening accidentally, you should "deselect" a block of text once you have finished altering it. Click the insertion point somewhere else in your document. The text will be deselected, losing its highlighting.

## Writing with Write

You can use what you have learned on these pages to type in a letter to one of your friends. Write will automatically start a new line each time you reach the right-hand margin. If you want to start a new line before you reach the right-hand margin, press the **Return** key. Use the selection and insertion techniques to correct any mistakes you make as you go along.

# More about Write

Once you have typed your text onto a Write page, you can change it until it is just the way you want. Altering a document like this is called editing.

## Choosing a style

Write's *Character* menu provides a variety of options for editing the appearance of your text. For example, you can choose from several text styles. To do this, select the text that you want to alter, then click on one of the *Character* menu commands shown in the chart below.

| **Bold** | Makes text thicker |
|---|---|
| **Italic** | *Makes text lean to the right* |
| **Underline** | <u>Draws a line under text</u> |
| **Regular** | Returns text to standard style |

When you select a style command, a small tick appears next to it in the *Character* menu. If you click on a style command with a tick next to it, the tick disappears, and the style is switched off. You can combine text styles by picking more than one style command.

| ✓ **Bold** | Ctrl+B |
|---|---|
| ✓ *Italic* | Ctrl+I |
| ✓ <u>Underline</u> | Ctrl+U |

*See what your text looks like when you combine these three styles.*

## Sizing your text

The *Character* menu also lets you alter the size of your text. To do this, first select the text you want to resize. If you want to make this text smaller, click on the *Reduce Font* command. To make it larger, click on the *Enlarge Font* command.

## The Paragraph menu

As well as altering the style and size of your text, you can choose how you want it to be positioned on your page. The borders that surround the text are called margins. By selecting a block of text, and then clicking on a command in Write's *Paragraph* menu, you can place the text in different positions between the left and right margins, as shown below.

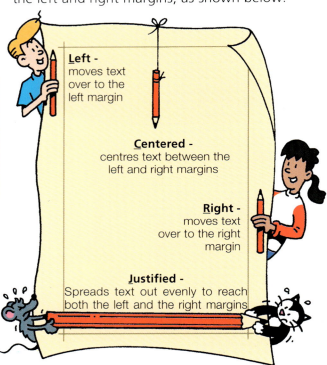

**Left** - moves text over to the left margin

**Centered** - centres text between the left and right margins

**Right** - moves text over to the right margin

**Justified** - Spreads text out evenly to reach both the left and the right margins

## Spacing out your text

You can also use Write's *Paragraph* menu to choose how much space there is between one line of your text and the next. Select the text block whose line-spacing you want to alter, and choose from the *Single Space*, *1½ Space*, or *Double Space* commands in the *Paragraph* menu.

To return text to Write's standard layout (single spaced text, aligned to the left margin), select the text and click on the *Normal* command in the *Paragraph* menu.

18

## The ruler

Instead of using menu commands, you can edit your Write document using the "ruler". If you pick the *Ruler On* option from Write's *Document* menu, a horizontal ruler appears across the top edge of the Write window.

Each of the ruler's boxes and bits performs the same function as one of Write's menu commands. Select the text you want to alter, and click on the part of the ruler which creates the effect you want.

**The Write ruler's parts.**

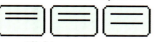
Clicking on one of these boxes sets the spacing between one text line and the next.

Clicking this box moves selected text over to the left margin.

Clicking this box positions text centrally between the side margins.

Clicking this box moves selected text over to the right margin.

Clicking this box spreads selected text evenly between the left and right margins.

## Using the Clipboard

You can move a block of text from one place in your document to another using the Windows Clipboard system. Select the text that you want to move. Pick *Cut* from Write's *Edit* menu. The text will be removed from your document and be placed out of sight on the Clipboard. Using the I-beam, move the insertion point to the text's new location. Pick *Paste* from the *Edit* menu and the text will be copied from the Clipboard back into your document.

## Copying your text

If you select a block of text and pick the *Copy* command from Write's *Edit* menu, the text will be copied onto your Clipboard without being removed from its original location. You can then use the insertion point and the *Paste* command to insert the copied text in other places in your document.

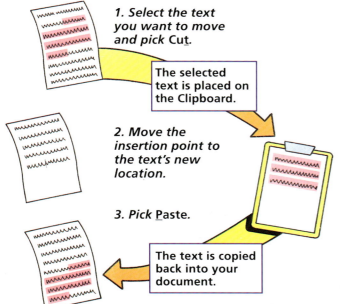

1. Select the text you want to move and pick Cu**t**.

The selected text is placed on the Clipboard.

2. Move the insertion point to the text's new location.

3. Pick **P**aste.

The text is copied back into your document.

### WARNING!
The Clipboard can hold only one chunk of information at a time. Cutting or copying something new onto the Clipboard deletes whatever was previously there.

## Clipboard Viewer

If you want to find out what is currently stored on your Clipboard, you can use Program Manager to find and run a program called Clipboard Viewer. This displays the contents of the Clipboard inside a window on your desktop.

*The Clipboard Viewer icon*

19

# Using dialog boxes

As you use a Windows application, you will come across some menu commands which end in three dots. Whenever you pick one of these commands, Windows 3.1 displays a questionnaire called a dialog box on your desktop. Dialog boxes let you enter information about what you want to do.

## Fonts

An example of a Windows 3.1 dialog box is the one you use in Write to choose a "font". A font is a complete set of letters, numbers and symbols of a particular appearance. As you create a document, you can choose from a range of fonts, to make your text look just the way you want. Each font has its own name.

*This picture shows a selection of the many different text fonts.*

## Write's Font box

You can pick a font before you type in your Write text, or select a block of existing text and change it to a particular font. In either case, you use a dialog box to enter your choice of font. Click on the *Fonts...* option in Write's *Character* menu. After a brief pause, Write's Font dialog box will appear on your desktop.

*This is Write's Font dialog box.*

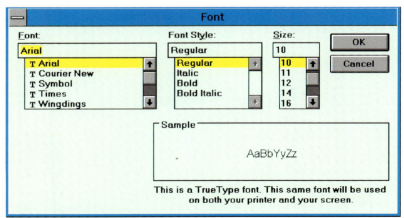

## Changing settings

Three smaller boxes inside the Font dialog box display the current text settings. They show the name of the font, and the style and size of the text (see page 18).

By scrolling through the list of possible settings beneath each of these three boxes, and clicking on a font, style and size of your choice, you can enter new text settings.

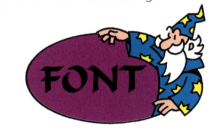

A sample of text in the font, style and size that you have specified appears in the Sample box at the bottom right-hand corner of the Font dialog box. If you are happy with your choices, click the *OK* button. The dialog box will disappear, and your new text settings will take effect.

# Dialog controls

Write's Font box is one of the many different dialog boxes you will encounter as you use the Windows 3.1 system. Some contain special gadgets, such as buttons, boxes or lists. You use each of these gadgets in a particular way to enter information.

*This pretend pizza order form gives you an idea of how some of the common dialog box controls work.*

**This is an OPTION BUTTON.** Click on it to select one of several options. A dot appears inside the circle next to the selected option.

**You can click on these up and down arrows to make a number setting larger or smaller.**

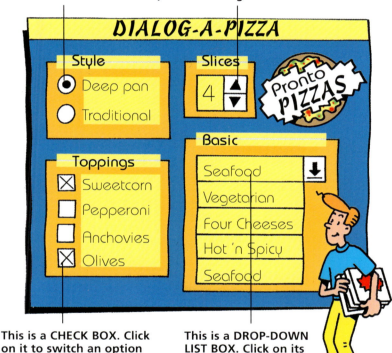

**This is a CHECK BOX.** Click on it to switch an option on or off. If an option is on, a cross appears in its box. You can select more than one check box option.

**This is a DROP-DOWN LIST BOX.** Click on its arrow button to open a list of options. You can then select one option by clicking on it.

### HELP!
To try out the various dialog box gadgets, you can follow the section on dialog boxes in the Windows Tutorial. Find out how to follow a particular section of the Windows Tutorial on page 45.

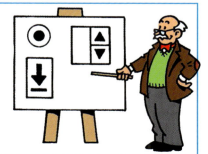

# OK or Cancel?

When you have selected new settings in a dialog box, you make your choices take effect by clicking on the box's *OK* button.

If you decide that you don't want to make the changes you have selected after all, you can abandon a dialog box by clicking on its *Cancel* button. The dialog box will vanish from the desktop, and your document will remain unchanged.

# Writing with Write

Use what you now know about Write's controls and commands to edit the letter that you typed in on page 17. Try aligning your address to the right margin. You could alter the font, style and size of parts of your text, or even use the Clipboard to rearrange the order of your letter.

# Whoops!

Write's *Edit* menu includes a command called *Undo*. Whenever you use the ruler, menu commands, the Clipboard or dialog boxes to edit your text, and then regret it, click on *Undo* to cancel your last editing step. Most Windows applications have an *Undo* command.

# Saving your work

When you have produced a document using an application, Windows 3.1 lets you store it so that you can return to it later. This is known as saving your work.

## Disks, drives and files

Inside your computer is a device called a hard disk, which can store lots of information. The hard disk sits inside a hard disk drive, which records information onto it.

Your computer stores each batch of information, such as a Write document, as a "file" on the hard disk. When you want to use a particular piece of information again, the hard disk drive retrieves the file you need.

## Floppies

A floppy disk is a small disk, cased in plastic, which can store files in much the same way as a hard disk. You insert a "floppy" into its disk drive through a slot in your computer.

If you save a file on a floppy disk, you can remove the disk from its drive and take the file away to use on another computer.

*This cutaway picture of a PC shows the main types of disk drive.*

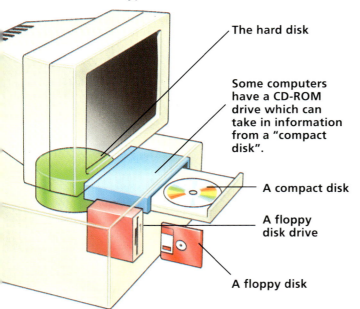

The hard disk

Some computers have a CD-ROM drive which can take in information from a "compact disk".

A compact disk

A floppy disk drive

A floppy disk

## The Save As box

Before you can save a document as a file on disk, you need to give it a name, and tell the computer where on disk you want to keep it. Windows applications have a dialog box, called a Save As box, which lets you enter these details when you save a document.

To find out how to use a Save As box, try saving the Write letter that you created on the previous pages. Pick the *Save As...* command from Write's *File* menu. The dialog box below will appear on your desktop:

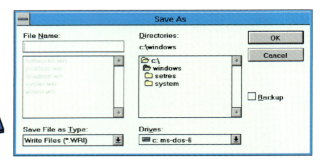

## Naming your file

To give your Write letter a name, click the insertion point into the box labelled "File Name" in the top left-hand corner of Write's Save As box. Then type in the name of your choice. You can give a Windows 3.1 file a name that is up to eight characters long. It cannot include spaces, or any of the characters shown below:

$$. : / \setminus [ \ ] * | < > + = ; , ?$$

A filename is usually followed by something called an extension. This consists of a full stop and a three character code. Each application has its own filename extension. Your computer can tell from an extension what type of file it is dealing with. Add the extension ".wri" to your filename to label your file as a Write document.

*The File Name box*

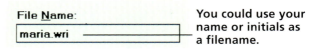

You could use your name or initials as a filename.

22

## Picking a drive

The next step when saving a file is to choose the disk drive that holds the disk on which you want to store your file.

Near the bottom of the Save As box is a box labelled "Drives". Click on the Drives box to see a drop-down list of all your PC's disk drives.

*The Drives box*

Drives:
- c: ms-dos-6
- a:
- b:
- c: ms-dos-6

**Each of your computer's drives is represented in the Drives box by a symbol labelled with a letter.**

To save your Write letter on the hard disk, pick the hard disk drive by clicking on it in the Drives list. It is represented by this symbol, and is usually labelled as the "c" drive.

## Directories

You can gather the files stored on a disk into groups. This is rather like organizing lots of paper documents into separate folders. It makes it easier to find a specific file later on. The "folders" on a disk are called directories.

The disk on which you are about to save your file may contain several directories, so you need to specify which one you want to store your file in before you can save it. Above the Drives box in the Save As dialog box is a box labelled "Directories". This displays a list of all the directories on the disk in the drive that you've selected. Each one is represented by a small folder symbol, labelled with a directory name.

## Picking a directory

To save your file in a particular directory, you need to find that directory's folder symbol in the Directories list and double-click on it.

You will find out on page 34 how to create a personal directory in which to keep your own work. In the meantime you should save your Write letter in the main directory on the hard disk, known as the hard disk root directory (see page 31). To open this directory, double-click on the folder symbol labelled "c:\" at the top of the Directories list.

*The Directories box*

Directories:
c:\
- c:\
- dos
- mouse
- temp
- windows

## Giving the OK

You have now told your computer what you want to call your file and where you want to store it. Click on the Save As box's *OK* button, and your computer will save your document. The Save As dialog box will disappear, and your document's filename will appear across the title bar of the Write window. A copy of your letter is now safely stored as a file in the root directory on the hard disk.

### HELP!

This box may appear on your screen when you try to save your document. This means that the directory you've picked already contains a file with the name that you've chosen. Click the *No* button, use the Save As box to give your file a different name, and try the *OK* button again.

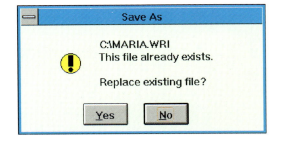

# More about files

On these pages, you will find out how to retrieve a file from disk when you want to use it. You will also learn how to keep your files up to date.

## The Open box

Retrieving a file from disk is known as opening a file. To enable you to find and open any file previously created using an application, Windows 3.1 provides a special dialog box, called an Open box.

Have a go at opening the file that you saved on page 23. Make sure that Write's window is open and active. If it still contains your letter, pick the *New* command from the *File* menu to clear away this document, so that you can try retrieving it from disk. Click on the *Open*... command in the Write window's *File* menu. Write's Open box will appear on your desktop.

*Write's Open box.*

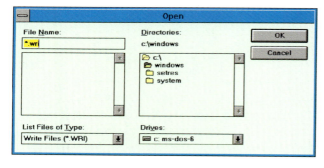

## Opening a directory

You use an Open box to tell your computer the name of the file you want to open, and where to find it. Your Write letter file is stored in the root directory on your PC's hard disk (see page 23). Use the "Drives" list inside Write's Open box to pick the hard disk drive. Then use the "Directories" list to open up the root directory, just as you did on page 23.

## Selecting a file

Once you have opened a directory, a list of filenames appears in the left-hand part of the Open box. This is an alphabetical list of all the files in the open directory that match the application you are using. Because you are using Write's Open box, the list will show all the files in the directory that end in ".wri".

Scroll through the list of filenames until you find the one you want. By clicking on your letter's filename, you can enter it into the "File Name" box at the top of the list.

Now that you've told your computer which file you want to open, and where to find it, click on the *OK* button. Your PC will retrieve the file from disk. The Open box will vanish, and your letter will appear in the Write window.

*The File Name box*

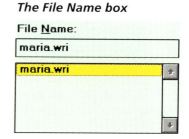

## The Save option

If you alter a document after you've retrieved it from disk, you may want to save the new version.

There is no need to use the Save As box, as you did on page 22, to save the new version of your document. Your file already has a name and disk location. Instead you can simply click on the *Save* command in the *File* menu. Your computer will automatically store the latest version of your document in its original disk location, under its original filename.

## Keeping up to date

As you work on a Windows document, you should use the *Save* command regularly to keep the version on disk "updated". This means that if your PC's power supply fails for any reason, you will be able to retrieve the most recent version of your document from disk.

### WARNING!
When you use the *Save* command, your PC replaces the previous version of your document on disk with the new version.

If you want to keep both versions of a document, you need to save the new version as a separate file, using the *Save As...* command to give it a different filename. One way of naming a new version of a document is to add a number to the original document's filename.

## Closing a window

To stop a program running, you have to close its window. To do this you click on the control-menu box in the top left-hand corner of the window (see page 8). The window's "control menu" will appear. Pick the *Close* command from this control menu. As a speedy alternative, you can close a window simply by double-clicking on its control-menu box.

When you have finished your Write letter, and saved the latest version of it on disk, close the Write window.

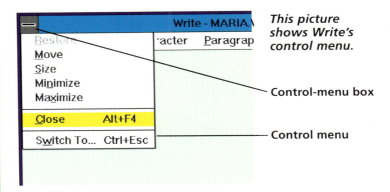

*This picture shows Write's control menu.*

— Control-menu box

— Control menu

## Saving current changes

When you try to close a window, a box may appear on your screen telling you that you have changed your document since the last time you saved it. Your computer is checking whether or not you want to save the latest document version before you close its window.

If you want to save the current version of your document over the previous version, click the *Yes* button. If you don't want to save the current version, click *No*.

If you want to keep both the previous and current versions, click the *Cancel* button to return to your document, and use the *Save As...* command to save the current version under a new filename.

*Write's "Save changes?" box*

# Paintbrush

This is the icon for Paintbrush, a Windows 3.1 application which lets you create pictures on screen. Use Program Manager to find and run the Paintbrush program. When the Paintbrush window appears on your desktop, maximize it so that you can take a closer look.

## Picking a canvas size

The main area of the Paintbrush window shows a canvas on which you can create a picture. You can specify the size of the canvas you want to use, and choose whether you want your picture to be in colour or black and white. To do this, pick *Image Attributes...* from the *Options* menu. The dialog box shown below will appear:

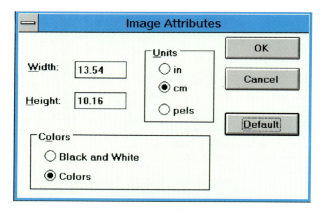

To set your canvas to a standard size, click on the *Default* button. If you want to paint with a variety of colours, make sure that the *Colors* option is selected. Then click the *OK* button.

Your canvas will now be slightly larger than the Paintbrush window's picture display area, so Paintbrush provides scroll bars to enable you to move your view across your canvas.

## Choosing colours

Paintbrush provides several different drawing tools and a range of coloured paints to use them with.

To choose colours for your picture, you use the multicoloured strip at the bottom of the Paintbrush window. This is called the Palette.

*Part of the Palette*

You can pick both a foreground colour to draw with, and a background colour to draw on. You will find out how each Paintbrush tool uses these two colours on the opposite page.

To pick a foreground colour, click on a colour in the Palette with the primary mouse button. To pick a background colour, click on a Palette colour with the secondary mouse button (see page 10). The box at the left-hand end of the Palette shows the colours you have chosen:

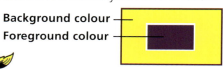

## The Toolbox

At the left-hand edge of the Paintbrush window is a panel of eighteen small pictures, called the Toolbox. You use the Toolbox to choose from Paintbrush's drawing tools, each of which creates a different effect on your canvas.

To select a tool, click on it in the Toolbox so that it is highlighted. You can then move it around the canvas using your mouse. Most tools appear in the picture area as a cross-shaped pointer, but some have their own particular pointer shape.

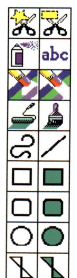

*This is the Toolbox panel.*

## Special effects

The picture below shows some of the effects you can create using different drawing tools and colours. Have a go at producing your own Paintbrush work of art!

You can use the Brush tool like a crayon, dragging it to make a mark on the canvas in the foreground colour.

These tools let you drag out different shaped outlines. By holding down the Shift key as you use a tool, you can use the Ellipse tool to draw a perfect circle, or the Box tool to draw a perfect square. The outlines appear in the current foreground colour.

The Airbrush tool sprays the foreground colour onto the canvas as you drag it around.

Dragging the Eraser tool over part of your picture rubs it out by colouring over it in the background colour.

As you drag the Color Eraser across the canvas, it replaces any areas of the foreground colour with the background colour.

Clicking the Paint Roller tool inside an enclosed area fills in that area with the foreground colour.

The Polygon tool lets you drag out a series of connected lines to create a many-sided shape called a polygon. The free end of the last line must join up with the free end of the first line to form a closed shape.

These tools let you drag out a filled-in shape. The border appears in the background colour, and the shape is filled in with the foreground colour.

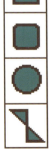

The Line tool lets you draw a straight line. Drag the cross-shaped pointer from where you want the line to start, to where you want it to end. If you hold down the Shift key as you drag the Line tool you can draw vertical, horizontal and 45° diagonal lines.

This tool lets you drag out a straight line and then bend it twice, by dragging, to create a curve.

## Changing your brush

You can change the width of the Brush, Eraser, Color Eraser and Airbrush tools. Click on the width you want in the Linesize box in the bottom left-hand corner of the Paintbrush window. You can also use the Linesize box to set the thickness of curves, straight lines and the outlines of shapes.

*The Linesize box*

27

# More about Paintbrush

Once you have drawn a Paintbrush picture, you can add text to it, or zoom in on part of it to add details. You can even cut bits out so that you can move or alter them.

## Adding text

To add text to your picture, select the Text tool from the Toolbox. As you move the pointer across the picture area, it will turn into an I-beam, like the one you used in Write. Position this I-beam where you want to add text to your picture, and click. An insertion point will appear, enabling you to type text onto your canvas in the current foreground colour.

**The Text tool**

## Paintbrush styles

Like Write, Paintbrush lets you vary the appearance of text. You can use Paintbrush's *Text* menu to select a font and text size, or to pick the bold, italic or underline styles. Paintbrush also has two extra text style options. The *Outline* command produces foreground coloured text with a thin outline in the background colour. *Shadow* produces foreground coloured text with a shadow in the background colour.

**The Outline style**

**The Shadow style**

## Changing your view

A standard Paintbrush window displays the Palette, the Toolbox, the Linesize box, and part of your canvas. But you can alter this standard view if you want.

If you pick *Zoom Out* from the *View* menu, Paintbrush displays your picture at a smaller scale, so that the entire canvas fits inside the picture area. You will find out on the opposite page why you may sometimes need to use this zoom out view. To return to the standard view, select *Zoom In* from the *View* menu.

To take a look at your picture without the Paintbrush controls around it, select the *View Picture* command from the *View* menu. To return to the controls, click anywhere on the display.

**A Paintbrush window showing the standard view.**

**A Paintbrush window showing the Zoom Out view.**

## Zooming in close

You can work in detail on a small section of your picture by picking *Zoom In* from the *View* menu. Your pointer will change into a small rectangular box. Use your mouse to move this box over the section of your picture that you want to look at in detail, then click. The picture area will display a close-up of the selected section, showing the tiny squares, called pixels, which make up your picture.

You can alter the picture section one pixel at a time. Click the foreground colour into a pixel using the primary mouse button, or the background colour using the secondary mouse button.

When you have finished adding details to your picture section, select *Zoom Out* from the *View* menu to return to the standard Paintbrush view.

**The Zoom In view**

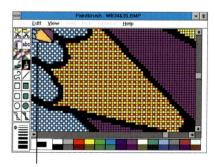

**This box shows the picture section at actual size.**

## The cutout tools

The Toolbox includes two "cutout" tools. You use these to outline a section of your picture so that you can move it to a new position on your canvas, or alter it using the commands in Paintbrush's *Pick* menu.

*These are the two cutout tools.*

 The Scissor tool lets you draw a wavy outline to create an irregularly shaped cutout section.

 The Pick tool lets you drag out a rectangular outline to create a box-shaped cutout section.

## Moving part of picture

Once you have cut out a section of your picture, you can drag it to a new position on your canvas. When the section is where you want it, click somewhere outside its outline and Paintbrush will place the section back on the canvas. Alternatively, you can choose the *Cut* or *Copy* command from the *Edit* menu to place a cutout section on the Windows Clipboard. Pick *Paste*, and a copy of the cutout will appear in the top left-hand corner of the picture area. You can then drag the cutout section wherever you want on the canvas and click it into place.

### WARNING!

When you click a cutout picture section into place, any part that doesn't fit within the picture display area is trimmed off. If you want to avoid this happening, select *Zoom Out* before you use a cutout tool. You can then use the Pick tool and the *Cut*, *Copy* and *Paste* commands to move cutout sections without damaging them.

## Using the Pick menu

You can use the commands in Paintbrush's *Pick* menu to alter the appearance of parts of your picture. Use one of the cutout tools to outline the section you want to alter, then click on a *Pick* menu command.

*This diagram shows what the Pick commands do.*

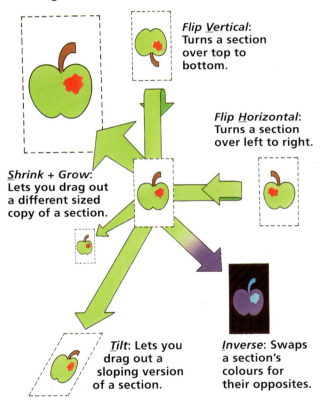

*Flip Vertical*: Turns a section over top to bottom.

*Flip Horizontal*: Turns a section over left to right.

*Shrink + Grow*: Lets you drag out a different sized copy of a section.

*Tilt*: Lets you drag out a sloping version of a section.

*Inverse*: Swaps a section's colours for their opposites.

## Saving your artworks

You can keep a Paintbrush picture on disk just like any other Windows document. Use *Save As...* to store your picture in the root directory on the hard disk (see pages 22 and 23). Because you are saving a Paintbrush file, you need to use the Paintbrush filename extension, which is ".bmp". When you have completed and saved your picture, close Paintbrush's window.

# Using File Manager

As you save more and more files on disk, it's important to keep track of where each one is stored. Windows 3.1 has a program, called File Manager, which helps you do this.

Use Program Manager to find and run the File Manager program. It is usually found in a program group called Main. When the File Manager window opens on your desktop, maximize it to take a closer look.

*This is File Manager's icon.*

## Avoiding accidents

File Manager lets you move files from one place to another on disk, change their filenames, or even delete them completely. You need to take care not to do any of these things by accident.

File Manager has a safety system to prevent accidental alterations. As soon as you open its window, check that this safety system is switched on. To do this, pick the *Confirmation...* command from the *Options* menu. Make sure that the dialog box which appears is filled in like the one below, with a cross in each of its five check boxes. Then click the *OK* button. File Manager will now ask for confirmation whenever you try to move, delete or alter a file.

*File Manager's Confirmation box*

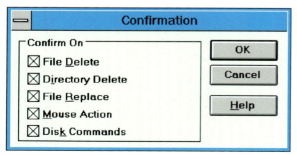

## Tidying the display

To help you find your way around File Manager for the first time, it's a good idea to convert its window to a standard layout.

Hold down **Shift** and press the **F5** key. One or more windows will appear in a stack inside the File Manager window. These are called directory windows.

As a beginner, it's best to have only one directory window open at a time. So close all but one of the directory windows, using their control-menu boxes (see page 25).

Pick *Tree and Directory* from File Manager's *View* menu. This will divide the remaining directory window into two equal areas.

*Your File Manager window will now look like this.*

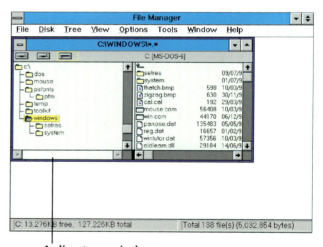

*A directory window*

## Using a directory window

Files are grouped into separate directories on disk (see page 23). A File Manager directory window enables you to look inside a directory to see what files it holds.

It's possible to have several directory windows open inside File Manager, but only one of these windows can be active at a time. You can find out on the opposite page what the various parts of a directory window are used for.

## The disk drive bar

Instead of a menu bar, a directory window has a bar containing several small symbols. Each symbol represents one of your computer's disk drives.

When you want to look at the contents of a particular disk, you select the drive which contains that disk by clicking on its symbol. Try clicking on the hard disk drive symbol (see page 23) to find out what files are stored on your hard disk.

*A directory window disk drive bar*

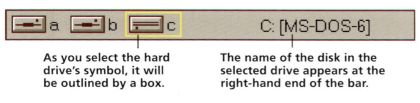

As you select the hard drive's symbol, it will be outlined by a box.

The name of the disk in the selected drive appears at the right-hand end of the bar.

## The directory tree

The left-hand side of a directory window shows a diagram, called a directory tree. This represents the arrangement of directories on the disk inside the selected disk drive. Files grouped together in a directory are often separated again into further directories. The directories within a particular directory are known as its subdirectories. The directory tree diagram shows this arrangement as a series of folders inside other folders.

To take a closer look at the tree layout, select *Expand All* from File Manager's *Tree* menu, and use the scroll bar at the right-hand side of the directory tree to move your view to the top of the tree.

## Roots and branches

Every disk has one main directory, called the root directory, which contains all the other directories on that disk. The root directory on the selected disk is represented by a folder symbol at the very top of the directory tree. Lines called branches run from the root directory symbol to other folder symbols, each representing a subdirectory inside the root directory. Some of these folders also have branches running to other folders, showing how they in turn are divided into subdirectories.

*A directory tree*

```
📁 c:\ ———— root directory
   ├── 📁 dos
   ├── 📁 mouse
   ├── 📁 psfonts
   │     └── 📁 pfm
   ├── 📁 temp
   ├── 📁 toolkit
   └── 📁 windows
         ├── 📁 setres
         └── 📁 system
```

## Directory contents

You will find out on page 32 how to use the directory tree to find and select the directory that you want to look inside. Once a directory is selected in the tree, the right-hand side of the directory window shows a list of its contents.

*A directory contents list*

| | | |
|---|---|---|
| 📁 setres | | 09/07/9 |
| 📁 system | | 01/07/9 |
| 📄 thatch.bmp | 598 | 10/03/9 |
| 📄 zigzag.bmp | 630 | 30/11/9 |
| 📄 cal.cal | 192 | 29/03/9 |
| 📄 mouse.com | 56408 | 10/03/9 |
| 📄 win.com | 44170 | 06/12/9 |
| 📄 panose.dat | 135483 | 05/05/9 |
| 📄 reg.dat | 16657 | 01/02/9 |
| 📄 wintutor.dat | 57356 | 10/03/9 |
| 📄 aldlearn.dll | 29184 | 14/06/9 |

## Paths

A directory window's title bar shows the "path" for the directory currently selected in the tree. This describes the route to the directory along the branches of the directory tree.

For example, if you wanted to look in the "system" directory inside the "windows" directory on the hard disk, you would need to open the hard disk root directory (labelled "c:"), open the "windows" directory inside that, and open the "system" directory inside that. The path for this directory would be written like this:

### C:\WINDOWS\SYSTEM

Each step in the path is separated by a backslash (\).

# Finding your files

Whenever you want to retrieve one of your documents from disk, you can use File Manager to find and open its file.

## Which disk?

To find a file, you first have to tell your computer which disk it is stored on. To do this, use the active directory window's disk drive bar, as described on page 31, to select the drive that holds the disk you want.

## Picking a directory

Once you have selected a drive, the active directory window will display a directory tree for the disk inside it. Search this directory tree to find the directory in which your file is stored.

Sometimes the directory tree doesn't show the subdirectories contained within certain directories. You might have to alter the tree's layout so that it includes a separate folder symbol for the subdirectory that contains your file. This is known as expanding the directory tree.

## Expanding branches

To expand the directory tree so that it shows a specific directory's subdirectories, select that directory by clicking on its folder symbol, and pick *Expand Branch* from File Manager's *Tree* menu. Alternatively, you can simply double-click on the directory's folder symbol. The directory's subdirectories will appear in the tree diagram.

**The Windows directory before and after it is expanded**

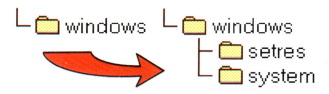

## Expanding tips

To help you remember which directories contain subdirectories, make sure there is a tick next to *Indicate Expandable Branches* in File Manager's *Tree* menu. A small "+" sign will appear inside the folder symbol of any directory that contains subdirectories which are not shown in the tree.

The easiest way to ensure that the directory tree displays the entire layout of directories and subdirectories, showing a separate folder symbol for each one, is to pick *Expand All* from File Manager's *Tree* menu.

## The contents list

When you have found the directory containing your file, click on its folder symbol to open it up. A list of the directory's contents will appear in the right-hand half of the directory window.

**The directory contents list**

**Each of your document files is represented by this symbol**

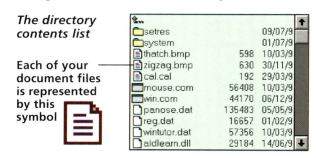

## Opening a file

Use the scroll bar at the right-hand edge of the directory window to look through the directory contents list. When you find the file you want, open it by clicking on its filename so that it is highlighted, and picking the *Open* command from File Manager's *File* menu. Alternatively, you can simply double-click on its filename.

As you open the file, the window of the application that you used to create it will appear on your desktop, containing your document.

# Finding lost files

The instructions on the opposite page only enable you to find and open a file if you can remember where it is stored. If you've forgotten where the file you want is kept, you'll need to use File Manager's *Searc**h**...* command to track it down.

# The Search box

To find a lost file, you first have to tell your computer which part of which disk you want it to search. If you can remember which directory the file you want is in, use File Manager's active directory window to find and select it. If you can't remember, select the root directory so that your computer will search the entire disk.

Once you have selected a directory, pick *Searc**h**...* from File Manager's *F**i**le* menu. The Search dialog box will appear on your desktop.

**File Manager's Search dialog box**

# Specifying a search range

The "Start *F*rom" box inside the Search dialog box shows the path for the directory you are about to search (see page 31). If you decide that you want your computer to search a different directory from the one currently selected in the tree, type the alternative directory's path in the Start From box. Make sure that there is a cross in the "S*e*arch all subdirectories" check box. This ensures that your computer will look through all the subdirectories of the directory that you've named.

# Entering a search name

The "Search For" box inside the Search dialog box lets you type in the name of the file that you're looking for. If you can't remember the exact filename, you can enter an approximate version. Substitute a "*" character in the place of any part of the name that you've forgotten. Your computer will try to find a filename which matches your approximation.

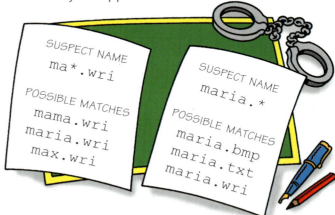

# Search results

Once you have entered a search range and name, click the *OK* button to start your search. File Manager will track down all the files inside the search range with filenames that match your Search For name.

A window will appear inside the File Manager window, listing the names of any files which match your search details. If you can see the file you are looking for in the Results window, you can open it up by selecting it and picking *Open* from the *F**i**le* menu, or by double-clicking on its name.

**The Search Results window**

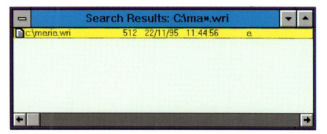

# Organizing your files

If you want to rearrange your files on disk, you can use File Manager to move them about. These pages tell you how to use the active directory window to organize your files.

## Your own directory

The best way of organizing your files so that they are easy to find is to create a directory of your own to keep them in. Have a go at creating a personal directory on your computer's hard disk. Select the hard disk root directory in the directory tree, and pick *Create Directory...* from File Manager's *File* menu. A dialog box will appear, enabling you to type in a name for your new directory. As with filenames, directory names can only have eight characters, and cannot include spaces, or any of the characters shown below:

. : / \ [ ] * | < > + = ; , ?

When you have entered a directory name, click the *OK* button. Your new personal directory will appear in the tree, as a subdirectory of the hard disk root directory. You can store all your future files inside this directory by selecting it whenever you use a Save As box (see pages 22 and 23).

## Source to destination

You can use File Manager to move a file from one directory to another on a disk. To do this, use the active directory window to take the file from its original disk location, known as its source, and put it in a new location, known as its destination. The diagram below shows how you use the active directory window to move a file.

*Moving a file*

**1. Make sure the destination directory is displayed in the directory tree. Expand the tree if necessary.**

**2. Open the source directory and find the file that you want to move in the directory contents list.**

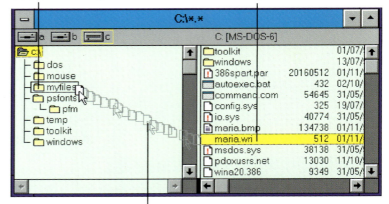

**3. Drag the file across onto the folder symbol of the destination directory. As you drag a file it appears as a small document symbol.**

**4. When the document symbol is correctly positioned over the destination directory, the directory is outlined by a box. Release the mouse button.**

Try moving the Write letter file that you saved on page 23, and the Paintbrush picture file that you saved on page 29, into your own directory on your computer's hard disk.

## Copying a file

You can create a copy of a file and put it in another directory without removing the original from its source directory. To do this, follow the same procedure as for moving a file, but hold down the **Ctrl** key as you drag the file into the destination directory. This will leave a copy of the file in both the source and destination directories.

## Disk to disk

File Manager even lets you transfer a file from one disk to another. This is useful if you want to copy a file from your hard disk onto a floppy disk, so that you can move it to another PC.

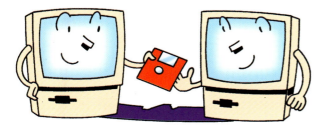

To copy a file from one disk to another, you first have to open up the directory you want to copy the file into. Use File Manager's active directory window to open this directory on the destination disk.

Next use the directory window to look for the file that you want to copy on the source disk. When you find the file, drag it onto the disk drive bar. Position it over the symbol of the drive which contains the destination disk, and release the mouse button.

*Copying a file to a different disk*

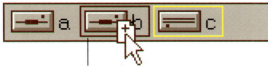

**When the file is positioned correctly, a black box will outline the destination drive's symbol.**

To move a file from one disk to another, rather than copy it, hold down the **Shift** key as you drag the file onto the destination drive's symbol.

## Using Re<u>n</u>ame

If you decide that you want to change the name of a file or directory, use the active directory window to find and select it. Then pick Re<u>n</u>ame... from File Manager's *F*ile menu. Use the dialog box that appears on your desktop to enter a new name, and click *OK*.

## Deleting files

If you want to get rid of a file completely, use the active directory window to find and select it. Then pick *D*elete from the *F*ile menu.

## Multiple selection

File Manager lets you handle several files at once. To do this, you need to select the files from the directory contents list, using the multiple selection technique shown below.

*Selecting multiple files*

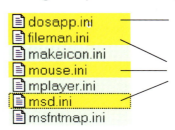

1. Click on the first file you want to select

2. Hold down the Ctrl **key and click on each of the other files you want to select**

Once you have selected them, you can move, copy or delete multiple files using the same techniques as you would for an individual file.

---

### WARNING!
Each time you move, copy or delete files, a box will appear on your desktop asking you to confirm your command. Always check the details in this box before you give File Manager the go-ahead by clicking *Y*es.

*A typical File Manager confirmation box*

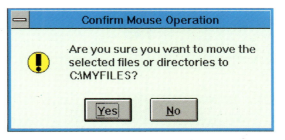

Never delete, move, or rename any files other than your own. They may be essential to your computer's proper functioning, or important to another user.

---

35

# Printing a document

Once you have created a document, you can use a printer to produce a copy of it on paper.

## On and On-line

Before you try to print a document, make sure that your printer is plugged in, connected to your computer, and switched on. You also need to check that the printer is "on-line", which means that it is ready to receive information from your PC. Usually you press an on-line button on the printer. A light comes on to show you that the printer is on-line.

## The Print box

Windows applications have a Print dialog box, which lets you give your PC the information it needs to print your document properly.

Have a go at printing out the letter that you created on pages 16 to 21. Open the Write window and open your letter file. Select the *Print...* command from Write's *File* menu. Write's Print box, shown below, will appear:

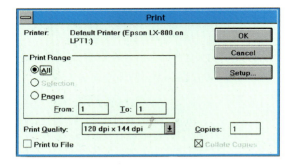

## How many copies?

The *Copies* setting inside a Print box lets you tell your computer how many copies of your document you want. To print a single copy of your letter, type "1" in the *Copies* setting box.

## Which pages?

If your document has several pages, the *Print Range* setting lets you specify which of these pages you want to print. To print your entire letter, select *All* in the *Print Range* setting box.

You are now ready to start printing. Click the *OK* button. The Print dialog box will vanish and a smaller box will appear on your desktop, confirming that your document is being printed.

## Printing problems

Your computer may be set up so that Windows 3.1 automatically runs a special program called Print Manager whenever you print a document. If anything goes wrong with the print-out, Print Manager displays a message on your desktop, advising you what to do to overcome the printing problem.

If you have difficulties printing your document, and Print Manager fails to help, run through the following check list:

**1-** *Is your printer plugged in and connected to the computer correctly?*

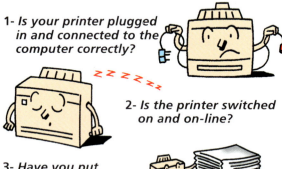

**2-** *Is the printer switched on and on-line?*

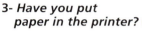

**3-** *Have you put paper in the printer?*

**4-** *Is your computer set up to use this kind of printer? Does the printer you are using match the one named in the Print dialog box?*

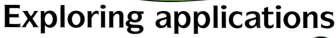

# Exploring applications

By working with Write and Paintbrush, you have come across the main parts of the Windows 3.1 system and used the standard Windows 3.1 techniques. You can now use what you have learned to explore other Windows 3.1 applications on your computer.

## Finding your way around

Approach unfamiliar applications step-by-step, using the techniques described in this book. If you need a reminder of how to perform a particular task, flick to the relevant page to refresh your memory. You could start your explorations by trying out the Windows 3.1 application called Notepad.

*This noticeboard shows how you can apply what you know to approach Notepad for the first time.*

### HELP!
As you explore a new application, make use of the instructions included in the Windows Help system. You can find out how to use these Help instructions on pages 44 and 45.

## Not quite Write

Some applications will seem very different from the ones you've used so far. They won't look much like Write or Paintbrush, and might be used for other things than creating documents. But you can still use your mouse skills to control these applications on your desktop, and your experience of menus and dialog boxes to explore what they can do.

For an example of a very different kind of Windows 3.1 application, try out a program called Solitaire, included in the Games program group. Solitaire's window lets you play a solo card-game on your Windows desktop.

*The Solitaire window*

① Find and run the Notepad program using Program Manager. **Pages 14&15**

② Use the Notepad window on your desktop to create a text document. **Pages 16&17**

③ Edit your document using menu commands and dialog boxes. **Pages 18-21**

④ If you want a copy of your Notepad notes on paper, use a printer to print them out. **Page 36**

⑤ When you have finished with Notepad, save your notes as a file on disk, and close the Notepad window. **Pages 22-25**

⑥ Use File Manager if you want to move, copy, or rename your Notepad files. **Pages 30-35**

# Windows 3.1 gadgets

These pages introduce some of the other handy applications included in the standard Windows 3.1 software.

Use the approach described on the previous page to explore each of these applications. They are usually found in a program group called Accessories.

## Notepad

Notepad enables you to jot down lists, reminders, or other straightforward text documents. You type your text onto a page within a window, using an I-beam and insertion point system just like Write's. Unlike Write, however, Notepad has only one font, and few editing options.

By choosing *Word Wrap* from Notepad's *Edit* menu, you can make sure that your text always fits within the window's side borders, as it does in the picture below.

*This is a Notepad window.*

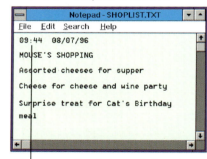

**To stamp the date and time in your notes, press the F5 key.**

If you want to save your notes as a file on disk, remember to use the Notepad filename extension, ".txt". To print out your shopping list or memo, pick *Print* from Notepad's *File* menu.

## Clock

The Clock application displays a clock-face inside a window on your desktop. You can make this clock-face as large or small as you like by changing the size of Clock's window. The *Settings* menu lets you choose between a clock-face with hands (analog) or with numbers (digital).

*The analog clock-face*

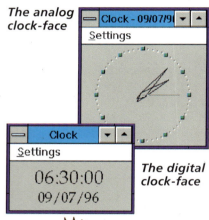

*The digital clock-face*

To pick a font for the digital clock-face, use the *Set Font...* command in Clock's *Settings* menu. If you want to hide the Clock window's title and menu bars, pick *No Title* from the *Settings* menu. To display them again, double-click anywhere on the clock-face.

You can choose to have the Clock window permanently on top of your desktop. To do this, pick *Always on Top* from Clock's control menu.

## Calculator

The Windows Calculator is useful if you have any sums to do. You operate it just like an ordinary calculator, using the pointer to click on its buttons.

*Calculator looks like this.*

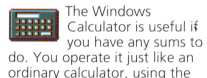

If you pick the *Scientific* command from the *View* menu, lots of extra buttons appear. You can use these if you need to carry out more complicated calculations.

## Calendar

 This application lets you create your own Windows calendar. When you first open the Calendar window, it shows a blank page listing the hours of the day. To add a reminder or appointment, simply type it onto this blank schedule. You can use arrow buttons beneath Calendar's menu bar to flick through similar schedules for other dates.

*Calendar's daily view*

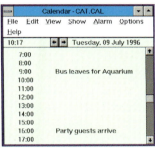

If you press the **F9** key, Calendar will display a monthly calendar. Use the arrow buttons to flick backwards or forwards through the months of the year. You can mark a particular date for special attention by clicking on it and then picking the *Mark...* command from the *Options* menu. If you double-click on a date, Calendar displays the schedule for that day.

*Calendar's monthly view*

You can create separate calendars for your home, school or work schedule, for birthdays, or for other important events. Save each calendar as a separate file on disk using the filename extension ".cal".

## Cardfile

 Cardfile lets you store information on an alphabetically ordered set of cards. It is ideal for noting down addresses, telephone numbers, or similar details.

To add a new card to a cardfile, press **F7**. A dialog box will appear asking you to enter an "index line" for the new card. This is the title by which the card will be alphabetically sorted. For instance, if you were creating a cardfile of friends' addresses, each card would have a friend's name as an index line.

Once you have typed in an index line for your new card, it will be slotted into its alphabetical position in your cardfile. You can then type whatever information you like onto the card.

***This Cardfile window shows a sample address file.***

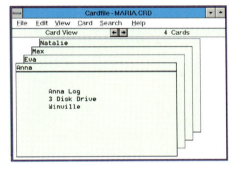

You can create as many cardfiles as you like. Save each one as a separate file on disk, using the filename extension ".crd". When you want to look at the information stored in one of your cardfiles, use the *Open...* command in Cardfile's *File* menu to retrieve it from disk.

To find a particular card, use the arrow buttons beneath the window's menu bar to flick through your cardfile. Alternatively, you can use the *Go To...* command in Cardfile's *Search* menu to specify the index line of the card that you want to look at. Cardfile will then retrieve the card automatically.

The *Print* command in Cardfile's *File* menu lets you print out one or all of the cards in a cardfile, so that you can have a copy of the stored information on paper.

# Organizing your desktop

Windows 3.1 lets you have several programs on your desktop at the same time. These pages tell you how to organize your desktop as it becomes crowded with windows and icons.

## Switching

There are all sorts of occasions when you need to run several programs. For example, if you were writing a story using Write, you might want to open a Paintbrush window to create illustrations for your story. You might also want to look in your Windows Notepad (see page 38) to find plot ideas that you jotted down earlier.

*This screen shows a busy desktop.*

As your desktop becomes crowded with windows and icons, it gets harder to find the program that you want to use next. You need to bring that program's window to the top of the desktop. This is known as switching.

Usually you can switch to a program by clicking on part of its window or, if it is running in minimized form, by double-clicking on its icon. But if you can't see either the program's window or its icon, you'll need to use one of the following special switching techniques.

## Using Alt+Tab

The first way of switching to a program which is running, but which you can't find on your desktop, is to use the **Alt** and **Tab** keys. Hold down the **Alt** key and press the **Tab** key. A box will appear in the middle of your screen showing the icon and name of a running program.

*The Alt+Tab switching box*

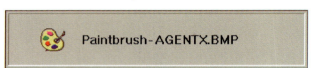

Keep **Alt** held down and press **Tab** repeatedly. Each of the programs that are running will appear in the box in turn. When the icon and name of the program you want appear, release the **Alt** key, and the selected program's window will jump to the top of the desktop.

## The Task List

The second way of switching to a hidden program is to use a box known as the Task List. Hold down the **Ctrl** key and press the **Esc** key. Release both keys and the Task List box will appear on your desktop.

*The Task List box*

The Task List shows a list of all the programs currently running on your desktop. You can look through this list and highlight the program that you want to use by clicking on its name. Click on the Task List's *Switch To* button to bring this program's window to the top of your desktop.

## Cascade and Tile

The Task List box contains several other useful buttons. Clicking the *Cascade* button gathers all the windows that are currently open into a tidy pile in the middle of your desktop. The active window lies on top of the pile. Clicking the *Tile* button changes the size of all open windows so that they fit neatly next to one another on your desktop.

Using either *Cascade* or *Tile* creates a space at the bottom of the display for the icons of any programs that are running in minimized form. If these icons become scattered around your desktop, you can line them up neatly by clicking the *Arrange Icons* button in the Task List box.

*Cascaded windows*

*Tiled windows*

## Clearing up

The more programs you have running, the slower your computer will work. So it's a good idea to close programs that you have finished with.

You can find out on page 25 how to close a window using its control-menu box. To close a program which is running in minimized form, click on its icon. The program's control menu will appear. Click on *Close*. The program will stop running and vanish from the desktop.

You can also use the Task List to clear away programs. Call up the Task List, select the name of the program that you want to close, and click on the *End Task* button.

## The ideal layout

Controlling several programs is easiest if you have only one program's window open at a time. All the other programs should be running in minimized form, lined up as icons along the bottom edge of the desktop.

To set up this layout, minimize all but one of the windows on your desktop. Then call up the Task List and click on its *Tile* button. This desktop layout gives you plenty of room in the window you are using. It also lets you switch quickly to other running programs when you need to.

To switch from one program to another, simply minimize the window on screen and double-click on the icon of the program you want to use next. Then use the *Tile* button to make the new active window a convenient size.

***This screen shows the ideal desktop layout.***

41

# Combining applications

Windows 3.1 lets you move information from one document to another. You can combine information created by different applications. As an example of this, these pages show you how to combine Paintbrush and Write to produce an illustrated text document.

## Moving a picture

Once you've inserted a picture in your Write letter, you can change its position so that your combined document looks just the way you want it to.

## Transferring information with Clipboard

The simplest way to combine Windows applications is to use the Clipboard, introduced on page 19, to transfer information between them.

Try inserting a Paintbrush picture in the Write document that you produced on pages 16 to 21. To do this, first use Paintbrush to produce an illustration for your letter. When you've finished your drawing, use the Pick or Scissor tool to cut it out (see page 29). Copy this cutout onto the Clipboard by picking *Copy* from Paintbrush's *Edit* menu. Then save your picture, as described on pages 22 and 23, and close Paintbrush's window.

The Clipboard now holds a copy of your Paintbrush picture. To insert it in your letter, open your Write file (see page 24). Position the insertion point where you want the illustration to appear in your letter. Pick *Paste* from Write's *Edit* menu. Your Paintbrush picture will be copied from the Clipboard into your document.

Pictures and text cannot appear on the same line in a Write document. The text of your letter will split so that it fits above and below the inserted Paintbrush picture.

*This diagram shows how you can use Clipboard to move information from one application to another.*

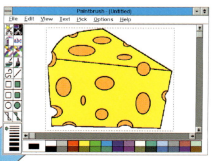

**1. Select the information you want to move, and use the Copy command to place it on the Clipboard.**

**2. Open the document in which you want to insert the information, and use Paste to copy it off the Clipboard.**

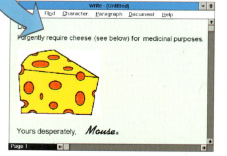

To move your picture to the left or right in your document, first select it by clicking on it with the I-beam. Then pick the *Move Picture* command from Write's *Edit* menu. A square pointer will appear near the middle of the inserted picture.

*Write's special square pointer*

By moving the square pointer with your mouse, you can shift your picture's outline across your document. Position the outline where you want the picture to be. Then click, and the picture will be moved to this new location.

To move your picture to a completely different place in your Write document, select it with the I-beam, and place it back on the Clipboard using the *Cut* command. You can then use the insertion point and *Paste* command to insert the picture wherever you want in your document.

## What size?

If you want to alter the size of your inserted picture, use the I-beam to select it, and pick the *Size Picture* command from Write's *Edit* menu. The square pointer will appear again. This time, you can use it to stretch or shrink your picture.

**Resizing an inserted picture**

**As you move the square pointer over one of the picture's borderlines, it will grab that borderline.**

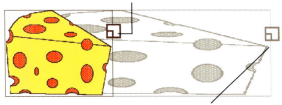

**Move the borderline to the position you want. Then click to make the picture appear at this size.**

## Editing your picture

You might want to alter your picture after you have inserted it in your letter. To do this, select the picture with the I-beam and pick *Edit Paintbrush Picture Object* from Write's *Edit* menu. Alternatively, you can simply double-click on the picture with the I-beam.

A Paintbrush window containing your picture will appear. Use the Paintbrush controls to make any alterations. When you have finished, pick the *Update* command from the Paintbrush window's *File* menu. This tells your computer to replace the copy of the picture in your Write document with the altered version. Pick *Exit & Return to...* from the Paintbrush window's *File* menu to return to your document.

## Saving a combined document

When you have finished your illustrated letter, use Write's Save As box to save it as a file on disk. Keep it with your other documents in the personal hard disk directory that you created on page 34. Because you have combined your letter and picture inside the Write window, use Write's filename extension, ".wri".

## Other combinations

You can combine many of the other applications on your PC in much the same way as Write and Paintbrush. You could try using the Clipboard to insert Notepad notes into a Calendar schedule, or to move Paintbrush pictures into a Cardfile to produce an illustrated address book.

If your PC has extra application software for creating sounds or animation, you can even insert noises and moving pictures into your Windows documents.

### HELP!

You can use an application's Help system to find out how to insert information created by other applications. Pages 44 and 45 explain how to use the Windows Help system.

# How to get help

Windows 3.1 includes a set of instructions, called the Help system. As you explore an application, you can use the information in the Help system to tackle unfamiliar commands and controls, or to remind yourself of specific Windows 3.1 techniques.

## Calling for Help

To get help with a particular program, you have to make sure that its window is active. Then either press and release the **F1** key, or pick the *Contents* command from the program's *Help* menu. A Help window showing the program's Help Contents page will appear on your desktop.

*This is the Contents page for Write's Help system.*

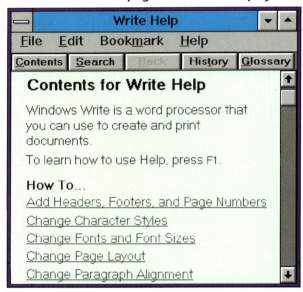

## Help topics

Each program's Help instructions are organized into separate topics, as in an instruction manual. The Help Contents page lists these topics, showing each one as an underlined title. Use the scroll bar to look through the Contents list and find a topic which sounds as if it will cover the information you need.

## Choosing a topic

Once you have found the topic you want, point at its title in the Contents list. The pointer will turn into a hand shape like this:

By clicking on a topic title with the hand-shaped pointer, you can jump to the Help section which explains that topic. Whenever you want to return to the Help Contents page to choose a new topic, click on the *Contents* button at the top of the Help window.

## The **S**earch button

Another way of finding information on a specific topic, is to use the Search option. Click on the Help window's *Search* button and the dialog box below will appear on your desktop:

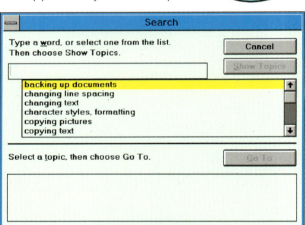

Follow the instructions in the upper half of the Search box to specify the subject about which you need information. You can type it in, or scroll through the list of available subjects to find and highlight the one you want.

Once you have specified a subject, click on the *Show Topics* button. All the Help topics relating to your chosen subject will appear in a list in the lower half of the Search box. Highlight the topic you want by clicking on it, then click on the *Go To* button to jump to that Help topic.

44

## The Glossary

Some of the more difficult computer words included in the Help instructions are underlined with a line of dashes. If you click the hand-shaped pointer on any of these words, a small box will appear containing a brief explanation of what that word means.

By clicking on the *Glossary* button you can browse through a list of all these tricky computer words in a window on your desktop. Click the hand-shaped pointer on any word in the Glossary window to find out what it means.

### HELP!
You can even use Help to find out how to use Help. Pick the *How to Use Help* command from the *Help* menu, or press the **F1** key twice in succession.

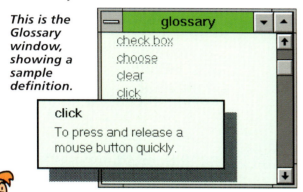

*This is the Glossary window, showing a sample definition.*

## The Windows Tutorial

As well as the Help system, Windows 3.1 includes a two-part lesson called the Windows Tutorial. The first part helps you learn the main mouse techniques (see page 11). The second part of the Tutorial, called Windows Basics, covers the skills introduced on pages 8 to 20 of this book.

To find the Tutorial, switch to Program Manager's window and pick *Windows Tutorial* from its *Help* menu. Press the **w** key to select Windows Basics.

You don't have to follow the lesson through from start to finish. You can flick backwards or forwards through its pages using the buttons at the bottom right-hand corner of the screen. By clicking on the *Contents* button, you can display the Tutorial Contents page and use a Topic button to jump to a particular section of the lesson.

## **B**ack and **H**istory

Clicking on the *Back* button in a Help window takes you back to the Help page that you were using last. You can use this button to go back one page at a time through the Help pages that you have already used.

By clicking on the *History* button, you can open a window that lists all the Help pages you have used. To jump back to a particular topic, double-click on its title in the History list.

*This is the Windows Help History window.*

The topics are listed in the order in which you looked at them, with the most recent last.

*This screen shows the Windows Tutorial Contents Page.*

# Windows 3.1 words

The list below explains some of the unusual words that you'll come across as you read or talk about Windows 3.1. Words printed in *italics* are explained elsewhere in the list.

If you come across any other unfamiliar Windows words, try looking them up in the Glossary included in the Windows Help system. You can find out how to use the Glossary on page 45.

**Active** The word used to describe a *window* that is currently in use.

**Button** Part of the *desktop* that you can "press" with the *pointer* to enter a command.

**Cascading** A way of arranging *windows* on the *desktop* so that they are neatly stacked.

**Clicking** Pressing the primary *mouse* button to "touch" an item on the *desktop*.

**Clipboard** The part of the Windows system which stores information temporarily, so that it can be transferred from one place to another.

**Closing** Removing a *window* from the *desktop* when it is no longer required.

**Desktop** The screen display used to control Windows 3.1.

**Dialog box** A rectangular area on the *desktop*, rather like a *window*, containing various controls used to enter choices.

**Directory tree** A diagram in the *File Manager* window showing how files are organized on disk.

**Disabled** The word used to describe a *menu* command or *button* which is temporarily unresponsive to *clicking*.

**Double-clicking** Pressing the primary *mouse* button twice in quick succession, usually to activate a *desktop* shortcut.

**Dragging** Pressing and holding down the primary *mouse* button to grab an item on the *desktop* in order to move it around.

**File Manager** The part of the Windows system used to find and organize files.

**Help system** The built-in instruction manual included in the Windows software.

**I-beam** The I-shaped *pointer* used to position the *insertion point* and select text.

**Icon** A small picture on the *desktop*, representing part of the Windows system.

**Inactive** The word used to describe a *window* which is displayed on the *desktop*, but is not currently being used.

**Insertion point** The flashing line showing the position where text is to be inserted in a document.

**Maximizing** Enlarging a *window* to fill the entire *desktop*.

**Menu** A list of Windows commands grouped together under a specific heading.

**Menu bar** A horizontal strip beneath a window's *title bar* used to select a particular *menu*.

**Minimizing** Converting a *window* to an *icon*.

**Mouse** A hand-held device used to control the *pointer*, and so operate the Windows system.

**Opening** Bringing a new *window* onto the *desktop*.

**Pointer** The movable on-screen arrowhead, controlled with the *mouse*, which is used to operate the *desktop*.

**Program Manager** The part of the Windows system used to find and run a particular program.

**Restoring** Returning a *window* to its original size and position on the *desktop*.

**Scrolling** Shifting a *window*'s view, using its scroll bars, until it displays a specific area of its contents.

**Switching** Using the *Task List* or special keystrokes to select a particular *window* from those on the *desktop*.

**Task List** A specialized *dialog box* for tidying the *desktop* or switching to a specific *window*.

**Tiling** A way of arranging *windows* on the *desktop* so that they fit neatly beside each other.

**Title bar** A strip across the top of a *window* showing its name.

**Wallpaper** The patterned layer covering the *desktop*.

**Window** A rectangular area on the *desktop* providing a workspace in which to use a particular program.

# PROJECTS FOR WINDOWS® 3.1
## FOR BEGINNERS

Program Manager

Recorder

### Philippa Wingate

### Illustrated by Derek Matthews, Jonathan Satchell and Nick Baxter

File Manager

Paintbrush

Sound Recorder

Cardfile

Write

Control Panel

Character Map

**Designed by Paul Greenleaf and Neil Francis**
Russell Punter, Non Figg and Rachel Wells
**Photography by Howard Allman**
**Technical Consultant: Richard Payne**
**Edited by Anthony Marks and Jane Chisholm**

# Contents

49  What is this section about?

50  A reminder of Windows 3.1 basics

52  Changing your Windows 3.1 display

54  Customizing your desktop

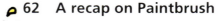

56  Super screen savers

58  A Write reminder

60  More news on Write

62  A recap on Paintbrush

64  Design your own wallpaper

66  Greetings and invitations

68  The personal touch

70  Outlines and stencils

72  All change

74  Mouse mats

76  Stickers and scenes

78  A picture address book

80  Character maps and codes

82  Invent your own quiz game

84  Finding a hidden message

86  Interactive storytime

88  Macro magic

90  Cartoon fun

92  More Windows 3.1 words

# What is this section about?

This section of the book shows you how to use the applications included free with Windows 3.1 software to tackle a variety of projects. These projects include customizing your Windows 3.1 display with new colours and patterns; making personalized stationary and greetings cards and creating cryptic codes and quiz games.

The main applications you will need to use are Control Panel, Write, Paintbrush, Cardfile, Character Map, Recorder and Object Packager.

## Versions of Windows

The projects in this section of the book are demonstrated using Windows 3.1 software.

You may have Windows® 95 installed on your computer (see pages 93 to 138). Many of the applications used in this section are included in Windows 95, so you can still complete many of the projects. Some, such as Character Map and Cardfile are exactly the same as in Windows 3.1. The 3.1 application called Write is replaced in Windows 95 by WordPad and Paintbrush is replaced by Paint.

Some applications, such as Recorder and Object Packager, are not included in Windows 95. This means that you will be unable to tackle the projects in which these applications are required.

***Tackle the projects with these versions of Windows.***

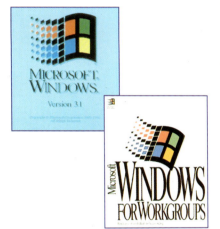

## Using this section

This section of the book includes some brief reminders of how to operate the main Windows 3.1 applications.

Each project is described with clear, step-by-step instructions. The projects get more complicated towards the end of this section, so it's a good idea to work your way through from beginning to end.

## Essential equipment

To complete many of the projects in this section all you need is a computer and Windows software. This section assumes that your Windows 3.1 software has been installed in a "typical" way. The project instructions are written for a right-handed mouse user.

To print pictures and letters, you will need a printer. If you don't have a colour printer, make sure you have pens or paints to decorate your print-outs.

If you want to send project files to your friends, you'll need floppy disks to transfer the files.

***This is the only equipment you'll need to tackle most of the projects in this book.***

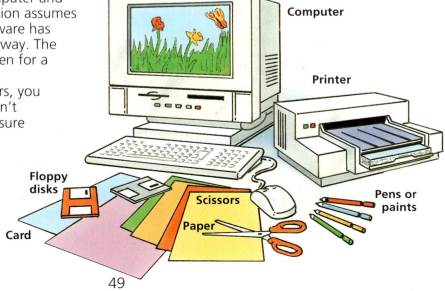

49

# A reminder of Windows 3.1 basics

These two pages include a brief reminder about the different parts of a Windows 3.1 display, how to control a window and how to open and close an application.

All this information is explained in greater detail in the first section of this book.

## Windows, icons and your desktop

A basic Windows 3.1 display is made up of windows, icons and a background layer called the desktop. The picture below shows you some of the main parts of a Windows 3.1 display and tells you their names.

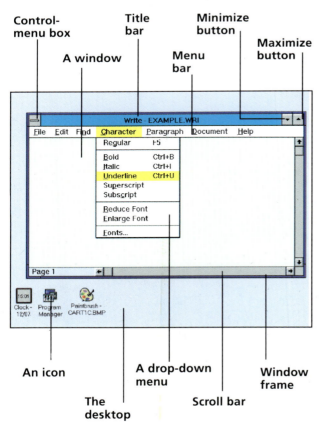

## Program Manager

When you first start up Windows 3.1, a window called Program Manager appears on your screen. If it appears as an icon at the bottom of your screen, double-click on it to open the window.

**This is the Program Manager icon.**

All the instructions for the projects in this book start from Program Manager. For these instructions to work properly, you need to open Program Manager's *Options* menu and click on *Minimize on Use*, so that a tick appears beside it, as in the picture below.

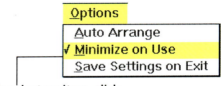

To select an item, click on it in the menu.

## Opening an application

All the applications on your computer are grouped together in program groups inside the Program Manager window.

**This is a program group icon.**

To open a program group, double-click on its icon. A new window will open inside Program Manager. It will contain the icons of all the applications in that particular group.

Each standard Windows application has a different icon. An icon usually gives you an idea of what its application is used for. For example, this icon is for File Manager, which is an application used to organize the files on your computer. The icon looks like a filing cabinet.

To open an application, simply double-click your pointer on its icon.

50

# Re-sizing a window

When an application opens, a window appears on your screen containing the work-space in which you use the application. You can change the shape of the window by clicking on its frame and dragging it into the shape you want.

To make a window fill your whole screen, click on its Maximize button.

*This window is being re-sized to a smaller size.*

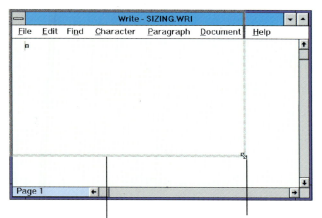

This outline shows you the new size of the window.

With this re-sizing pointer, drag the window into the shape you want.

# Minimizing applications

You can have several applications running on your computer at once. To make sure that you have enough space on your desktop to use an application properly, it's a good idea to minimize the windows of other applications. To do this, click on their Minimize buttons. They will appear as icons at the bottom of your screen. They are still running, and you can "restore" them to their former size, by double-clicking on their icons.

# Closing an application

If you have finished using an application and want to close it down completely, select *Exit* in the application's *File* menu. Another, quicker way of closing an application is to double-click in its control-menu box.

# Directories

All the files stored on a computer's hard disk are grouped together in directories. Make a new directory for the files you will create while doing the projects in this book. This will keep them separate from all the other information on your computer.

# Creating a new directory

To create a "projects" directory, open the File Manager application by double-clicking on its icon in Program Manager. Inside its window there will be one or more windows. Close all but one of these windows. Select *Select Drive* in the *Disk* menu and in the dialog box highlight the hard disk drive (usually the C drive). The window will now display the directories on the hard disk.

Click on the folder symbol at the top of the list which has C:\ written next to it (see below). Select *Create Directory...* in the *File* menu. A Create Directory dialog box will appear. In the *Name* box, type PROJECTS and click OK. A projects directory will appear in the list. Find out how to put files into this directory on page 58.

*File Manager's window with a projects directory*

The C:\ folder symbol

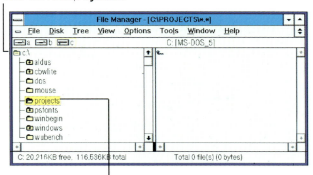

Your new directory appears in this list.

# Take care

Make sure that you don't delete or change any files already stored on the hard disk of the computer you are using.

51

# Changing your Windows 3.1 display

If you have a colour monitor, the desktop, windows and icons which make up a Windows 3.1 display will be multicoloured. If you have a black and white monitor, the display will be black, white and shades of grey. You can change the appearance of your display using the programs found in the Control Panel application.

## Control Panel

Control Panel is usually found in the program group called Main. Open it by double-clicking on its icon in the Program Manager window.

   *This is the Control Panel icon.*

## Things to avoid

When using Control Panel avoid the following programs: Network, Ports, Keyboard, International, 386 Enhanced, Drivers. They won't alter the appearance of your display, and changing them could cause problems with your computer hardware.

**Avoid these icons in Control Panel.**

## Changing colour schemes

To change the colour schemes of the windows and desktop that make up your Windows 3.1 display, double-click on the Color icon in the Control Panel window.

   *This is the Color icon.*

In the Color window that appears, open the *Color Schemes* list. It contains a selection of colour combinations, with names like Arizona, Tweed or Hotdog Stand. Try one out by highlighting its name in the list. The sample display below the list will change to show you what your chosen colour scheme looks like.

*The sample Windows display in this Color window is showing a scheme called Patchwork.*

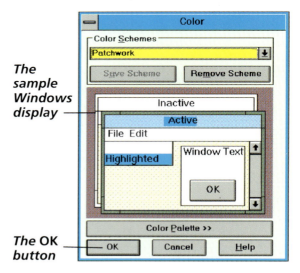

When you have found a scheme you like, click the *OK* button. The Color window will close and the display will show your new colours.

52

## Choosing your own colours

If you don't like any of the existing Windows colour schemes, you can create your own. In the Color window, click on the *Color Palette*>> button. The window will extend to show a palette of colours.

***The Basic Colors palette***

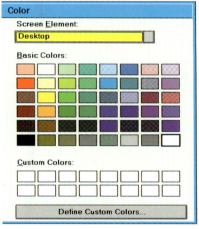

Click on any element of the sample Windows display, such as the "Active Title Bar" or the "Menu Bar". The name of the element you have selected will appear in the *Screen Element* box. Now choose a new colour for this element by clicking on any of the coloured squares in the *Basic Colors* palette.

## Mixing colours

Like an artist, you can mix up your own selection of dazzling new colours.

To do this, click on an empty square in the *Custom Colors* section. Click the *Define Custom Colors...* button. A dialog box appears containing a multicoloured square. Select the colour in any part of the square by clicking on it. To add this colour to your palette, click the *Add Color* button. To close the Custom Colour Selector box, click the *Close* button.

***The Custom Color Selector box***

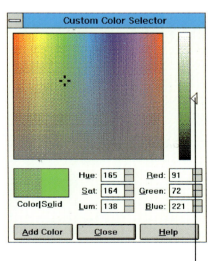

Drag this pointer up and down to change the brightness of your new colour.

## Saving a scheme

When you have designed a colour scheme that you are happy with, you need to save it. In the Color window, click the *Save Scheme* button. A dialog box appears. Type in a name for your scheme, such as Blue Boomerang or Peachy Pig Pink and click *OK*.

## Displaying a scheme

To display your colours on screen, close the Color window by clicking the *OK* button at the bottom left-hand corner of the window. Your personal colour scheme will automatically appear on the screen.

## Black and white

If you have a black and white monitor you can still change the appearance of your display. There are different shades and textures to choose from in the *Color Palette* dialog box.

Some of the schemes in the *Color Schemes* list begin with the letters LCD. These combinations are specially designed for use on monochrome monitors and laptop computers. Try some of them out using the technique described above.

# Customizing your desktop

There are other ways in which you can change the Windows 3.1 display. You can change the pattern that decorates the desktop using the Control Panel application.

## How to see your desktop

To make sure that you can see the desktop of your Windows 3.1 display, double-click on the Control Panel icon in Program Manager.

 This is the Desktop icon. Double-click on it and the Desktop window will appear. In this window there is a section called Wallpaper. Open up the *File* list and highlight *(None)*.

**The Wallpaper section of the Desktop window**

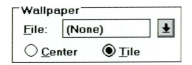

When you click *OK* in the top right-hand corner of the Desktop window, you will be able to see the desktop at the back of your screen.

## Colouring your desktop

To change the colour of your desktop, use the Color program in Control Panel. You can read about how to change the colour elements of your display on page 52 and 53. Select the desktop on the sample Windows display and assign it a new colour in the *Colour Palette*.

## Patterns on your desktop

The patterns which you can choose to decorate your desktop are made up of small patterns repeated hundreds of times to fill your screen.

In the section of the Desktop window called Pattern, open the *Name* list. This shows you all the desktop patterns provided by Windows.

***The Pattern section of the Desktop window***

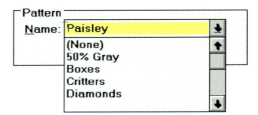

To try out one of the patterns, such as Boxes or Scottie, highlight its name in the *File* list. Click the *OK* button and your desktop background will immediately change.

***Two of Window's desktop patterns.***

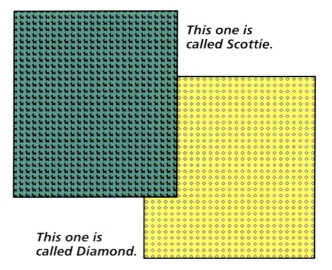

*This one is called Scottie.*

*This one is called Diamond.*

## How to design your own desktop pattern

If you don't like any of the existing desktop patterns provided in Windows 3.1, you can design your own. In the Desktop window, open the *Name* list in the Pattern section and select *(None)*. Click the *Edit Pattern...* button and a dialog box will open.

In the Edit Pattern dialog box there are two empty boxes. The larger one is covered with lots of invisible squares.

When you click anywhere in this square with your pointer, a small black square will appear. If you click on it again, the small black square will disappear.

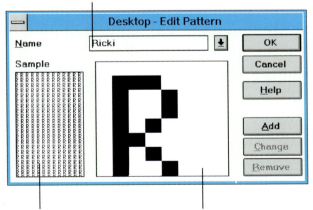

*This is the Edit Pattern dialog box.*

The name of your pattern.

This is the Sample box which shows you what your pattern will look like.

This is the box in which you draw your pattern.

Using this technique create new shapes and patterns by adding black boxes. As you change the pattern, you can see the effect it will have on your desktop in the box called Sample.

## Changing existing patterns

You can also change some of the existing desktop patterns. Select one of them and then click on *Edit Pattern...* Using your pointer, alter the pattern of the black squares.

*A selection of the patterns you can create.*

**You can use a letter.**

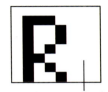

The box in which the pattern is drawn.

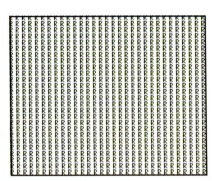

**Stripes look good.**

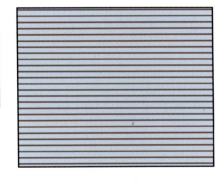

## Naming your pattern

When you have created a pattern that you like and want to keep, give it a name in the *Name* box, such as Stripes or Rings. Then click the *Add* button.

To close the Desktop - Edit Pattern dialog box, click the *OK* button. When you do this, you will immediately see your new pattern covering the desktop.

# Super screen savers

If you leave the same image displayed on your screen for a long time, it becomes permanently imprinted on the screen glass. This is called screen burn. To avoid it, you can use a program called screen saver, which replaces the image with a moving picture after a certain amount of time. Windows 3.1 provides a selection of different moving images that you can alter and personalize.

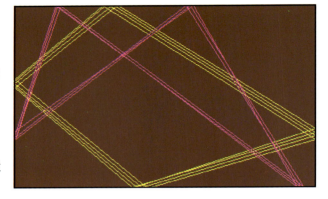

*This screen saver is called Mystify.*

## Turning on a screen saver

To choose a screen saver, double-click on the Control Panel icon in Program Manager. In the Control Panel window, double-click on the Desktop icon. There is a section of the Desktop window called Screen Saver. Open the *Name* list and you will find a list of screen savers available on your computer.

*This is the Screen Saver dialog box*

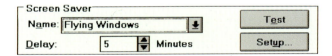

Try out one of them, say Flying Windows, by highlighting its name and then clicking on the *Test* button. If you use the Flying Windows screen saver, your screen will change to show lots of Windows logos rushing towards you.

*A screen showing Flying Windows screen saver*

## Stopping a screen saver

Screen savers are designed to disappear from the screen the moment you move your mouse or press any of the keys on the keyboard. Stop the test demonstration of a screen saver by doing either of these things.

## Setting a delay time

You can instruct your computer to start a screen saver automatically when you leave it unused for a certain amount of time. By clicking on the upward or the downward arrows on the right-hand side of the *Delay* box, you can alter the number of minutes your computer is idle before the screen saver is activated.

## Making changes

You can alter the colours and speed of some of the screen savers. To do this, highlight the screen saver you want to alter in the *Name* list. Click the *Setup...* button and a Setup dialog box will appear.

**This is the Mystify Setup dialog box.**

Make sure *Active* is selected.

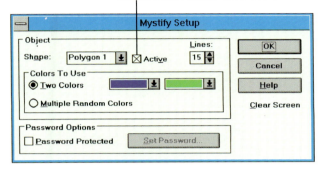

With the Mystify screen saver, for example, you can change the shape, colour and the number of lines which make up the shapes, called polygons, that appear on your screen.

You can decide whether the screen goes black when the screen saver starts or whether the polygons gradually black out the screen. When you have selected your preferences, click *OK*.

## Personal messages

If you choose to use the Marquee screen saver, you can write a message that will travel across your screen. Select a colour for the letters and the background. Type in your message in the *Text* box section. You can also choose the speed at which the words will travel. Finally, click *OK*.

**This is the Marquee Setup dialog box.**

## Passwords

In the Setup boxes of each screen saver you are given the option of putting a password on your screen saver. This means that when the screen saver comes on it will remain "locked" on the screen until you type in a special password.

It's not a good idea to put a password on your screen saver. You might forget the password and nobody would be able to use the computer until a computer expert unlocked the screen saver.

Click your pointer in the box beside *Password Protected* in the *Password Options* section until there is no cross in the box.

**This is the Password Options section.**

Make sure that there isn't a cross in this box.

## Ready to go

When you have selected the screen saver you want, click the *OK* button and close the Control Panel window by double-clicking in its control-menu box.

Your screen saver is now activated. Whenever you leave your computer for the period of time you have specified, the screen saver will appear.

57

# A Write reminder

You'll need to use Window 3.1's Write application in many of the projects in this book, so here's a reminder of some of its main features. To open Write, double-click on its icon in Program Manager.

***This is the Write icon.***

A window opens containing a blank page. A flashing cursor in the left-hand corner indicates where your text appears when you start typing.

***This is a Write window.***

Type a filename in the *File Name* box. It can have up to eight letters or numbers. All Write files have the extension .WRI. So select *.WRI in the *Save File as Type* box. In the *Drives* list highlight the disk drive which contains the disk you want to save your file on.

***Floppy disk drives have icons like this beside them.***

***The hard disk drive (usually the C drive) has an icon like this.***

To put your file into your projects directory (see page 51), double-click on the C:\ folder at the top of the *Directories* list. In the list that appears, double-click on the projects directory and then click *OK*.

This method of saving a file is similar to the technique you will use to save and store any file created in a Windows application.

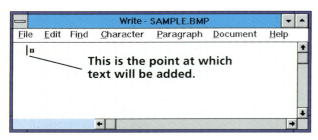

## Saving a Write file

When you have typed in some text, such as a letter or a story, you should save your Write document. Open the *File* menu and select *Save As...* The following dialog box will appear.

***A Save As dialog box***

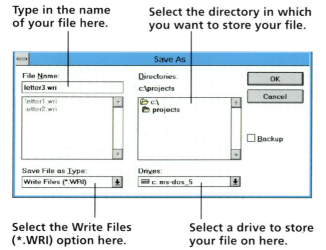

## Printing out a Write file

To print out a Write file, you need to have a printer installed and connected to your computer. Make sure that it is switched on and "on line", which means that it is ready to receive data from your computer.

Select *Open...* in Write's *File* menu. In the dialog box highlight the name of the file you want to print. Click *OK* and the document will appear in Write's window.

Select *Print Setup...* in the *File* menu. Check that the type of printer you are using is specified in the Printer section. In the Paper section, check that the size of the paper you are using is highlighted. Then click *OK*.

Select *Print...* in Write's *File* menu. If your document has more than one page, specify which pages you want to print. Enter the number of copies of your document you want. Finally, click *OK* to begin printing.

## Letterheads

You don't have to type your name and address at the top of every letter you send. You can store this information in a Write document called a letterhead.

## Creating a letterhead

Open a copy of Write and type in the information you want in your letterhead. This usually includes your name, address, telephone and fax number, but you may want to include other information too.

*A selection of printed letterheads and notepaper*

## Arranging text

You can arrange your letterhead information wherever you like on the page. To arrange any text, you must highlight it first. To do this, click your cursor at the beginning of the block of text you want to arrange and drag it to the end. Release the mouse button, and your text will appear highlighted, like **this**.

Highlight your letterhead information in this way, and in the *Paragraph* menu select *Left*, *Right* or *Centered*, depending on where you want your text to appear on the page.

## Saving your letterhead

When you are ready, select *Save As...* in Write's *File* menu. Give your file a name (letrhead.wri, for example). Place it in your projects directory and save it.

To write a letter, open letrhead.wri and type in your message underneath the letterhead information. Select *Save As...* in the *File* menu and give your letter a new filename (such as letter.wri). This will ensure that your letterhead file remains unaltered.

## Brighter letters

When you print out a letter, you can add colour and patterns to it with pens or paints. In the picture below, the letterheads have been printed on coloured paper. Bright patterns and borders have been added. You can make your own notepaper by printing your letterhead file onto several sheets of paper and adding a handwritten note.

# More news on using Write

You can use Write to create leaflets or newsletters. By exploring the different styles and shapes of text available and varying the size and position of your text, you can produce professional-looking documents.

## Using different text styles

One way of making text easier to read and understand is to use different text styles to emphasize important information. Write's *Character* menu provides a selection of text styles from which you can choose. Each one alters the appearance of text on the page, making it stand out from ordinary type. The different styles available are:

**Bold**, which makes text darker.

*Italic*, which makes text lean to the right.

<u>Underline</u>, which puts a line underneath text.

To use any of these styles, highlight the block of text you wish to alter (see page 59). Then select *Bold*, *Italic* or *Underline* in the *Character* menu.

**A letter showing different text styles in Write**

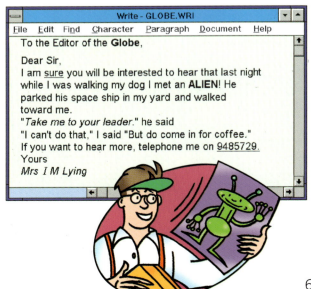

## Fonts

A font is a set of letters, numbers or symbols which have a unique shape and appearance.

THIS IS A FONT CALLED "BOSANOVA".

This is a font called "Briquet".

Stored on a computer is a selection of fonts that you can use to produce a document. Some fonts are provided with Windows 3.1 software, but you can also increase the range of fonts on your computer by buying extra software.

## Trying out different fonts

Open Write and type in some text. Highlight the text you want to change to a different font. In the *Character* menu select *Fonts*... A Fonts dialog box opens like the one below.

**A Fonts dialog box**

The *Font* list ———   Change the size of your text here.

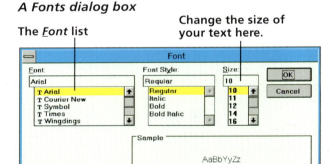

A sample of the selected font

If you select a font in the *Font* list, a sample of it appears in the Sample box. When you have found one you like, click *OK* and your text will appear in the new font.

You can also change the size of highlighted text by changing the number in the *Size* section of the Font dialog box. The higher the number, the larger your text.

## This text is size 18.

This text is the same font, but size 12.

# Making your own newsletter

Newspapers use a variety of different text styles and fonts. You may also have noticed that the text is usually arranged in narrow columns. You can use all these techniques to produce a newsletter like the one shown here.

## A narrow column of text

To create a narrow column of text, select *Ruler On* in the *Document* menu. A ruler appears at the top of your page. At the left-hand end of the Ruler is a triangular marker. This indicates the left-hand edge of your text column.

At the right-hand end of the ruler is another marker marking the right-hand edge of your text column. Click your cursor on it and drag it toward the left-hand side of your page. Using the measurements on the Ruler, position this triangle at the column width you require.

Now, when you type in your news story, it will appear in a neat column.

*A narrow column of text in Write*

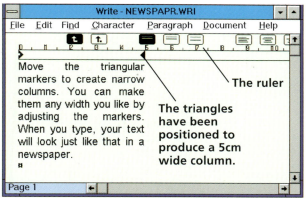

Move the triangular markers to create narrow columns. You can make them any width you like by adjusting the markers. When you type, your text will look just like that in a newspaper.

The ruler

The triangles have been positioned to produce a 5cm wide column.

## Justified text

Many newspapers use justified text. This means that the words in each line have been spaced out to fill the width of the column. To make your text justified, highlight it and select *Justified* in the *Paragraph* menu.

To make your newsletter more colourful, you can use felt-tips or stick in photographs.

## Finishing off

When you have printed out a selection of stories for your newsletter, paste them onto a large sheet of paper. Add lines to divide the columns of text and draw some pictures. When it is ready, photocopy and distribute your newsletter.

# A recap on Paintbrush

This is the icon for Paintbrush. You can read all about this application on pages 26 to 29, but here is a brief reminder of how to use it.

### A Paintbrush window

**The Toolbox has 18 drawing tools that create different effects.**

**This is the canvas area where you draw your picture.**

**A scroll bar**

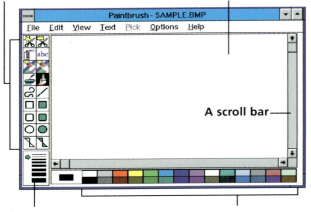

**The Linesize box allows you to select the width of your tools.**

**The Palette of colours**

## Sizing your canvas

To create a canvas of a particular size, select *Image Attributes...* in the *Options* menu. A dialog box appears like the one below:

**Enter size here.**

**Select your units here.**

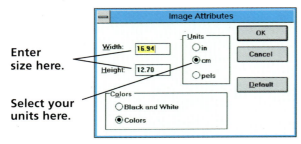

Type in the width and height of the canvas you require in the boxes. Make sure that centimetres is selected in the *Units* section. When you click *OK*, your canvas changes size.

If the canvas you are working on is too large to fit in Paintbrush's window, scroll bars will appear. By clicking on them, you can move around the whole canvas area.

## Choosing new colours

There are two main types of colour in Paintbrush: the foreground colour and the background colour. The foreground colour is the one you use to draw things. The background colour is the colour of the canvas on which you are drawing.

To pick a foreground colour, click on a colour in the Palette with your left-hand mouse button. To select a background colour, click with your right-hand mouse button. The box at the left-hand end of the Palette shows the colours currently selected for the foreground and background.

### Part of the Paintbrush Palette

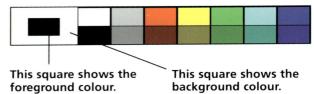

**This square shows the foreground colour.**

**This square shows the background colour.**

## Creating a picture

You can use any of the tools in Paintbrush's Toolbox to draw a picture. To select a new tool, click on its icon in the panel. To paint with it, drag your cursor over the canvas area. The best way to find out how all the different tools work is to experiment with them. Some of the more complicated tools are explained in greater detail in the projects where you need to use them.

62

## Erasing mistakes

You can correct any mistakes you make when drawing a Paintbrush picture. Highlight the  Eraser tool and move it over the area you want to erase.

**This is the Eraser tool icon.**

Alternatively, select *Undo* in the *Edit* menu, to undo everything you have done since you chose a new tool or colour.

## Saving a picture

To save a Paintbrush picture, select *Save As...* in the *File* menu. The dialog box below appears.

**The Save As dialog box**

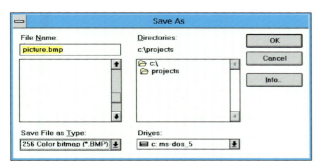

Give your picture a filename. Paintbrush filenames are always given the extension .BMP, so select *.BMP in the *Save File as Type* box. Place it in the projects directory and save it.

## New pictures

When you want to start a new canvas, simply select *New* in the *File* menu. A new canvas will automatically appear. It will be exactly the same size as the one you used previously.

## Printing out a picture

If you have a printer installed and connected to your computer and it is on line, you can print out a Paintbrush picture. To do this, select *Open...* in the *File* menu. Select the name of the file you want to print and click *OK*. Select *Print...* from the *File* menu. A Print dialog box appears, containing a selection of print options.

**This is the Print dialog box.**

**For the best quality printing, select *Proof*.**

**In this section you can choose to print a small area of your picture, or all of it.**

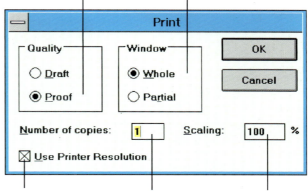

**Make sure that *Use Printer Resolution* is selected here.**

**Choose the number of copies you require here.**

**Use the *Scaling* section to enlarge or reduce the size of your picture.**

To make sure that your picture is printed as clearly as possible, select *Proof* in the *Quality* section. Make sure that *Whole* is selected in the *Window* section. This will ensure that all of your picture is printed, not just the area you can see in the Paintbrush window.

Type in the number of copies of your picture you want to print. Use the *Scaling* section to specify the size at which you want your picture to be printed out.

When you are ready, click the *OK* button to begin printing.

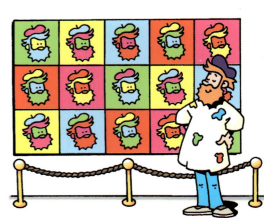

63

# Design your own wallpaper

You can cover your desktop with a layer of patterns or pictures called wallpaper. Choose a wallpaper from the patterns Windows 3.1 provides, or design your own.

## Choosing a new wallpaper

To choose a wallpaper for your screen, double-click on the Control Panel icon in Program Manager. Then double-click on the Desktop icon. In the Desktop window there is a Wallpaper section.

To ensure that the wallpaper you are about to choose appears all over the back of your screen, click in the circle beside *Tile* until a dot appears.

**The Wallpaper section**

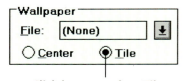

Click here to select *Tile*.

Now open the *File* list which contains the names of the Windows 3.1 wallpapers. They have names such as cars.bmp or zigzag.bmp. Try out one of them by highlighting it and clicking *OK*. The Desktop window will close and the new wallpaper will appear at the back of your screen.

**These screens show two of the Windows wallpapers**

This one is called leaves.bmp.

This one is called world.bmp.

## Customizing

To alter a Windows wallpaper, open a copy of Paintbrush. Select *Open...* in the *File* menu.

In the dialog box that appears, select the windows directory in the *Directories* section. Then, in the File *Name* section, select the name of the wallpaper you want to alter. When you click *OK*, part of that wallpaper will appear on your canvas. You can add colours and patterns to it.

## Color Eraser

A useful tool for customizing wallpaper is the Color Eraser. Select it by clicking on its icon in the Toolbox.

**This is the Color Eraser icon.**

The Color Eraser allows you to change the colours in a picture without altering the pattern. For example, if you don't like the blue areas of a wallpaper design, select that blue in the Palette with your left-hand mouse button. Select the colour you would like to replace it with, say red, with the right-hand mouse button. Then, hold down the left-hand button and, with your cursor, shade over the wallpaper design on your canvas.

**Using Color Eraser**

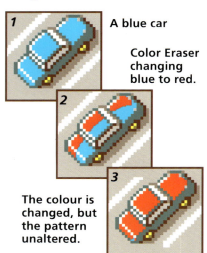

A blue car

Color Eraser changing blue to red.

The colour is changed, but the pattern unaltered.

Make sure that the original wallpaper file remains unaltered by saving your new wallpaper file under a different filename.

# Make your own wallpaper

You can design your own wallpaper using Paintbrush. A wallpaper appears on your desktop in tiles. The number of tiles that are needed to cover the desktop depends on the size of the canvas you use to create a wallpaper. If you draw on a small canvas (say, about 2cm by 2cm), it will be repeated many times to cover your desktop. If you choose a larger canvas (say, 6cm by 6cm), it will only be repeated a few times.

Open Paintbrush and select *Image Attributes...* in the *Options* menu. Enter the measurements of the canvas you require and click *OK*.

**Two sample wallpaper designs**

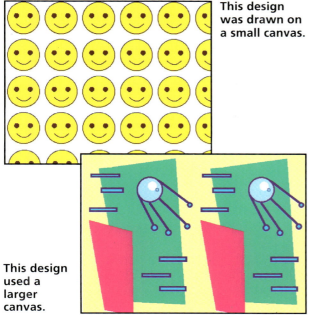

This design was drawn on a small canvas.

This design used a larger canvas.

Design a tile of wallpaper using any of the tools and colours Paintbrush offers. The Paintbrush window below shows a large tile of wallpaper.

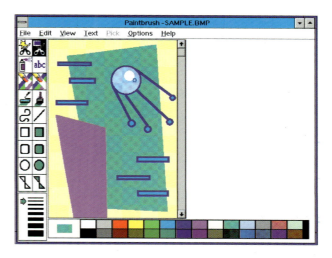

## Naming wallpaper files

When you have finished your wallpaper design, you need to save it. Click on *Save As...* in Paintbrush's *File* menu. Give your wallpaper a filename with a .BMP extension. Put it in the directory on your hard disk called windows and save it. Close Paintbrush by double-clicking in its control-menu box.

## Redecorating

To "paste" your wallpaper onto your desktop, open Control Panel and double-click on the Desktop icon. In the Wallpaper section, open the *File* list and select your newly named wallpaper file in the windows directory. When you click *OK*, your design will appear on screen.

# Greetings and invitations

Use Paintbrush to create pictures that you can mount on cardboard to make greetings cards and party invitations.

## Getting started

Open Paintbrush and select *Image Attributes...* in the *Options* menu. Specify a canvas that is about 12cm wide and 17cm high. Click *OK* and your canvas will appear.

When you draw your picture, use the scroll bars (see page 62) to fill the whole of your canvas.

**Some pictures drawn in Paintbrush**

## Outlined shapes

If you don't have a printer that prints in colour, create a design made up of outlined shapes that you can colour in after the picture is printed out. These are the icons for the tools which create outlined shapes.

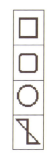

**A section of Paintbrush's Toolbox**

Give your shapes a clear outline by selecting a wide tool width in the Linesize box.

**This picture uses many of the outline tools.**

## Lettering in Paintbrush

This is the icon for the Text tool. You can use it to add text to a picture. There is a selection of different fonts, text sizes and styles to choose from. (You can read more about fonts and styles on page 60.)

To add text to a picture, select the Text tool. Open the *Text* menu and you will see the options of *Bold*, *Italic* or *Underline*. If you select *Fonts...*, a dialog box will appear in which you can alter the font and size of your text. Click on your canvas and start typing.

**You could make a card using different fonts and sizes.**

## Mistakes

If you want to change some text in a Paintbrush picture, use the Eraser tool to rub it out and then start again.

If you make a mistake while you are typing, you can use the back-space key to erase the mistake, then retype your text correctly.

## Zoom in

If you want to draw a picture carefully and precisely, try using a technique called "zooming in".

When you select *Zoom In* in the *View* menu, your pointer becomes a rectangle. Move this rectangle to the area of your picture you want a closer look at. Click, and the display will change to show that area in more detail.

When you are ready, select *Zoom Out* in the *View* menu to go back to the normal view of your canvas.

## Finishing touches

When the picture for your greetings card is finished, select *Save As...* in the *File* menu. Give your file a name (say, card.bmp), place it in the projects directory and save it.

Print out your picture onto a piece of paper. Mount it on a piece of cardboard that has been folded in half. Use paints, coloured pencils or felt tips to colour it in.

*Some cards for a birthday party*

## Making changes

This is the Brush tool's icon. When you have zoomed in on an area of a picture, you can use this tool to add detail to your picture, square by square. If you want to correct a mistake in a picture, add squares of the background colour by clicking in the squares with your right-hand mouse button.

*Looking at a detail of a picture using* Zoom In

**This box shows you the area you are altering, at its normal size.**

**The magnified area of your canvas**

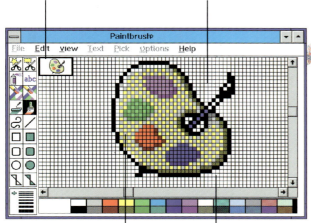

**Click on each square or drag your pointer over them to add colour.**

**Add background colour if you want to delete mistakes.**

# The personal touch

Many companies have a symbol or picture, called a "logo", which helps people to identify them or their products. Using Paintbrush you can create your own distinctive logo.

## Creating a logo

Open a copy of Paintbrush by double-clicking on its icon in Program Manager. Select *Image Attributes...* in the *Options* menu. Create a canvas about 4cm in width and 4cm in height, and then click *OK*. Now draw your logo, using any of the tools and paints.

*Here is a selection of different logo ideas.*

M*A*X

MARIE

TOM

When you have created your logo, select *Save As...* in the *File* menu, give your file a name (say, logo.bmp), place it in the projects directory and save it.

*Some logos on letterheads and personal cards*

## Using your logo

You could add your logo to the letterhead you created on page 59. Open the Paintbrush file containing your logo and select the Scissor tool.

*This is the Scissor tool icon.*

Use it to draw a dotted line around your logo, as shown below. Select *Copy* from the *Edit* menu. Close this copy of Paintbrush by double-clicking in its control-menu box.

*Cutting out your logo*

The cutting line created by the Scissor tool — This is the area that will be cut out.

## Inserting a logo

Open your letterhead file and click your pointer at the top of the page. Select *Paste* from the *Edit* menu. When your logo appears, highlight it and use the commands in the *Paragraph* menu (see page 59) to position it in the middle of your page, or on the left- or right-hand side. In a Write document, text can't appear on the same line as a picture.

## Personal Cards

A great way to give people your address and telephone number is on a personal card. To make one, open a copy of Paintbrush. Select *Image Attributes...* in the *Options* menu and specify a canvas that is about 9cm wide and 5.5cm high.

This is the icon for the Rectangle tool. Use it to draw a rectangle around the edge of your canvas to form an outline. Paste a copy of your logo onto the card using the technique described on page 68. Type in your address and phone number using the Text tool.

When you have finished, select *Save As...* in the *File* menu. Give your file a name, place it in the projects directory and save it.

*Here is a sample card.*

## Cards galore

By copying your personal card a number of times, you can produce a printed sheet of cards that you can cut out and give to your friends. Open the file containing your card and use the Pick tool to cut around it. Select *Copy* in the *Edit* menu.

**This is the Pick tool icon.**

Next, you need to create a new canvas to paste your card onto. Select *Image Attributes...* in the *Options* menu and create a canvas about 20 cm wide and 18cm high. When the canvas appears select *Zoom Out* in the *View* menu.

Your whole canvas will appear in the Paintbrush window. Select *Paste* in the *Edit* menu. A rectangle with crossed lines on it will appear. Click your pointer on the canvas outside this rectangle and a copy of your card will appear. If you select *Paste* again, a new rectangle will appear on top of your card. Click and drag this rectangle into position beside your first card.

**Placing six cards onto a canvas**

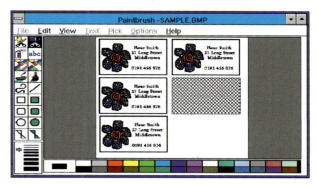

Repeat this process until you have six cards on your canvas. Now select *Zoom In* in the *View* menu. Select *Save As...* in the *File* menu. Give your file a new name (say, sixcard.bmp), place it in the projects directory and save it.

## Printing out

Print out the file with your six cards onto a piece of paper. You can use colourful paper or use pens and paints to add colour to your cards.

Glue the paper to a sheet of thin cardboard. When it is dry, carefully cut out the cards.

**Decorate your card with pens, pencils or paints.**

69

# Outlines and stencils

With Paintbrush's Text tool you can create outlined letters. Print them out and colour them in, or make them into stencils to decorate your possessions.

## Outlined letters

To create outlined text, open a copy of Paintbrush and select the Text tool. In the *Text* menu, choose the font, size and style of the text you want to use. Also in the *Text* menu, select *Bold* and *Outline* so that tick marks appear beside them.

**Paintbrush's Text menu**

Choose white as your foreground colour and black as your background colour. Type in some outlined letters using the keyboard. When you have finished, change your background colour to white and foreground colour to black.

**A sample of outlined text**

## Thicker letters

To make the outlines of your letters thicker, drag a rectangle around your letters with the Pick tool. Select *Copy* in the *Edit* menu and then select *Paste*. A copy of your letters will appear in the top left-hand corner of your canvas.

**A copy of your lettering**

With your pointer, drag this copy almost exactly over the top of the other letters. You will see that when it is almost, but not quite, over the top, the letters look twice as thick. Release your mouse button to position the letters.

**The copy is right beside the original.**

If the letters of your text are too close together, use the Scissor tool to cut carefully around each one. Click on it, and drag it slightly away from its neighbour.

## What is a stencil?

A stencil is a design that is cut into paper or plastic. You dab paint into the cutout shape to leave a pattern when the stencil is lifted off.

You can use outlined letters created in Paintbrush to make a stencil to decorate a folder, a pencil tin or a mug.

***Some of the things you can decorate with stencils.***

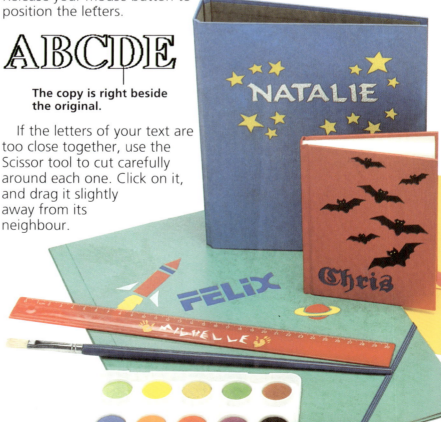

## Making a stencil

First measure the size of the area you want to stencil. Open a copy of Paintbrush, and select *Image Attributes...* in the *Options* menu. Specify a canvas that is the same size as the area you want to stencil. Now, when you design your stencil, you will be able to see exactly how much of the object it will cover.

When you have finished your stencil design, select *Save As...* in the *File* menu. Give the file a filename (stencil.bmp for example), place it in your projects directory and save it.

## Printing out

Print out your file onto the thickest paper you can use in your printer. Stencils get soggy when you use paint on them, so the thicker the paper, the longer they will last.

On this page, you can find out how to use a Paintbrush stencil to decorate the lid of a pencil tin.

## Stencilling

To stencil the lid of a pencil tin, you will need the following things: a sponge or crumpled cloth, ceramic paints, a piece of clear book-covering film, masking tape, a pencil tin, a ruler and an old saucer.

This is what you do:

1. Measure the lid of your tin and specify a canvas in Paintbrush that is the same size as it. Type your name in outlined type.

**This canvas is the same size as the tin's lid.**

2. Print out your name onto a piece of paper. Cut a piece of book-covering film that is slightly smaller than the lid of the tin. Tape the film over the letters on your print-out.

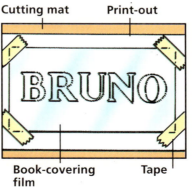

3. Using a craft knife, cut out all the letters. Make sure you cut through both the print-out paper and the book-covering film.

**Smooth out edges as you cut.**

4. Separate the print-out and the film and stick the film onto the tin. Add any middle parts of letters.

5. Put some paint onto the saucer. Dip the sponge into it, dab it on a paper towel, then over the letters.

6. Peel off the film carefully when the paint is dry.

# All change

The Paintbrush application allows you to alter pictures by adding details to them and making them larger or smaller.

## Dressing up

You can make different costumes for a figure drawn in Paintbrush. Open a copy of Paintbrush and draw a basic body shape. When you are ready, select Save As... in the File menu. Give your file a name (say, body.bmp), place it in your projects directory and save it.

**A basic body shape in Paintbrush, ready to be altered**

## All change

Draw an outfit for your figure. Select Save As... in the File menu. Give your file a new name (such as clown.bmp) and place it in your projects directory. This ensures that your body.bmp file remains unaltered.

To design another outfit, select Open... in the File menu and highlight the body.bmp file in your projects directory. Click OK and your basic body will reappear.

## Finishing touches

Print out your pictures onto paper. Glue thin pieces of cardboard to the back of the print-outs. When the glue is dry, use a sharp pair of scissors or a craft knife to cut around your figures. If you don't have a colour printer, use crayons or paints to colour in the clothes.

To make a figure stand up, glue a triangular piece of cardboard to the back of it.

***A selection of figures you could make***

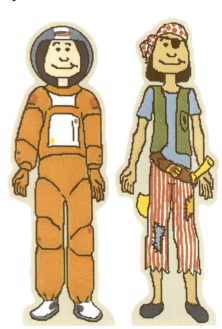

72

## Badges

You can use Paintbrush to design a selection of badges. Try making the logo you drew on page 68 into a badge. To find your logo, open Paintbrush and in the *File Name* list, highlight your logo.bmp file in the projects directory and click *OK*. The file will open.

Draw around your logo with the Pick tool and select *Copy* in the *Edit* menu. Now select *New* in the *File* menu. When a new canvas appears on your screen select *Image Attributes...* in the *Options* menu. Click on the *Default* button and then select *OK*. Finally select *Paste* in the *Edit* menu and a copy of your logo will appear on the canvas.

**Some badge designs based on logos**

## Shrink and grow

In your new Paintbrush file you can change the size and shape of your logo. With the Pick tool draw a rectangle around it. Select *Shrink + Grow* in the *Pick* menu. Your pointer will change into a cross-shaped cursor. Move it to a clear area of your canvas. Click the cursor on the canvas and drag a rectangular shape. When you release your mouse button, a copy of your logo will appear.

*Using* **Shrink + Grow**

**A picture**

**To make the picture bigger, drag a large rectangle.**

**To shrink it, draw a small rectangle.**

**These badges have been coloured in with felt-tip pens.**

## Undistorted

When you use *Shrink + Grow*, you can drag out a rectangle of any size and shape, and your logo will change to fill it. However, to make sure that your logo is not distorted (which means stretched too wide or too narrow), hold down the Shift key while you drag out the rectangle.

## Making badges

When you are happy with the size and shape of the logo for your badge, select *Save As...* in the *File* menu. Give your file a name (say, badge.bmp) place it in the projects directory and save it.

Print out your badge file onto a piece of paper. Glue a piece of thin cardboard to the back of the paper. Cut out your badge and colour it, as in the previous project.

To make your badge more hard-wearing, you could cover it with some clear book-covering film.

Use sticky tape to attach a safety pin to the back of the badge.

73

# Mouse mats

When using a computer mouse, you need to have a clean, flat surface to work on. You can buy a special mouse mat, or make your own using the Paintbrush application.

*Here are some ideas for mouse mats to make.*

## A graffiti mat

To create a mat with your name written on it like graffiti on a wall, open a copy of Paintbrush and maximize it to fill your screen. Select *Page Setup...* in the *File* menu. A dialog box appears. In the Margins section enter "0" for the *Top*, *Bottom*, *Left* and *Right* margins and click OK.

Select *Image Attributes...* in the *Options* menu and in the dialog box, specify a canvas 7cm wide and 10cm high. Then click OK.

## Brick laying

Select the Rectangle tool and choose white as your foreground colour and black as your background colour. In the top left-hand corner of your canvas area draw a brick.

**The Rectangle tool icon**

Select the Roller tool and choose a pale colour as your foreground colour. Click the inside of your brick to fill it with paint.

**The Roller tool icon**

## Creating a brick wall

To create a wall of bricks, use the Pick tool to cut around your brick. Select *Copy* in the *Edit* menu and then *Paste*. A new brick will appear on top left-hand corner of the canvas.

Drag the brick into position beside the first brick, with a small gap between them. Repeat this process until you have a full row of bricks.

## Copying rows of bricks

When you select *Zoom Out* in the *View* menu, your whole canvas will appear in the Paintbrush window. Use the Pick tool to draw around the row of bricks. Select *Copy* in the *Edit* menu and then select *Paste*.

A block covered with crossed lines will appear. Drag this box underneath your first row of bricks. When it is in position, click your cursor on the canvas outside the block. A new row of bricks will appear.

Select *Paste* again for another row of bricks to position and gradually fill your canvas with rows of bricks.

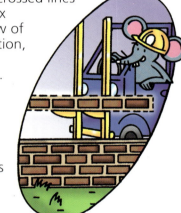

**Copying a row of bricks**

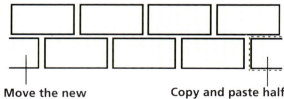

Move the new row of bricks across half a brick.

Copy and paste half a brick into the space at the end of each row.

## Writing on the wall

Select a wide width in the Line Width box and, with the Eraser tool, write your name across the wall. Add any decoration you like. Select *Save As...* in the *File* menu. Give your file a name, place it in the projects directory and save it.

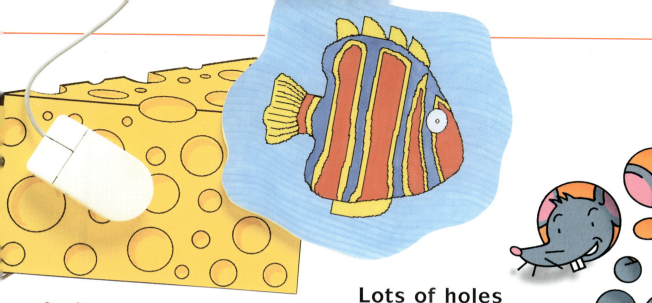

## A cheese mat

To make a cheese mat, open a copy of Paintbrush. Specify a canvas in the same way as described for the graffiti mat.

Use the Rectangle tool to draw a rectangle like the one in the picture below.

This is the icon for the Line tool. Use it to draw a line to form the top edge of the cheese.

Select the Curve Line tool icon and draw a line joining the top of the cheese to the rectangle. Use your cursor to curve the line. This is difficult. If you go wrong, select *Undo* in the *Edit* menu.

*This is what the finished cheese will look like.*

## Lots of holes

Use the Circle tool to draw holes in your cheese. The holes on the front of the cheese should be perfect circles. If you hold down the Shift key while you drag, you will get a circle. The holes on the top of the cheese should be squashed circles, called ellipses. You can draw them by dragging wide circles with your cursor.

## On the edge

Make sure that some of the circles you draw extend over the edge of the cheese. Where they fall outside the cheese, use the Eraser tool to rub out part of the circle and the edge.

## Finishing touches

When your picture is ready, select *Print...* in the *File* menu. In the Print box specify 275% in the *Scaling* section. Print the file onto a piece of A4 paper (about 21cm wide and 30cm high). You could use a sheet of yellow paper for the cheese mat. Use paints or pens to add colour to the print-out.

Finally, glue the print-out onto a piece of cardboard and cover both cardboard and print-out in clear book-covering film.

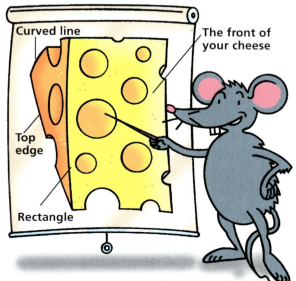

75

# Stickers and scenes

An aquarium filled with exotic fish, Photofit faces and fabulous fashion, are just some of the things you can create with a technique called clip-art. You will need to use the Paintbrush application.

## What is clip-art

Clip-art is a method of transferring a set of pictures from one Paintbrush window to another. You can treat the pictures like reusable stickers, sticking them onto different scenes and using them in different combinations.

## Two copies of Paintbrush

To tackle a clip-art project, you need two copies of Paintbrush open at once. First, open one copy of Paintbrush by double-clicking on its icon in Program Manager. Use your cursor to re-size (see page 51) this window until it covers the top half of your screen.

Go back to Program Manager and open another copy of Paintbrush by double-clicking on its icon again. Re-size this window to fill the bottom half of your screen.

## Active window

When you have two copies of the Paintbrush window open, click on the window you want to work on and it will become active, which means it is ready to use. The other window, which is not being used, is called inactive.

## Making stickers

Maximize one of the Paintbrush windows to fill your screen. Draw a selection of pictures, say a group of fish. This will be your stickers canvas.

*A selection of stickers*

Make sure the stickers are small, so that they can fit into a scene.

When you have finished, select *Save As...* in the *File* menu, give this Paintbrush file a name, place it in the projects directory and save it. Click the Restore button of this Paintbrush window.

## Setting a scene

Now create a scene for your stickers to appear in. Maximize your second Paintbrush window. Make sure that the background colour you select for this canvas is the same as that chosen for your stickers canvas. Design a scene.

This is your scenery canvas. Select *Save As...* in the *File* menu, give the file a name, place it in the projects directory and save it. Click the Restore button of this Paintbrush window.

*An aquarium scene*

76

# Copying and pasting

This is the icon for the Scissor tool. Use it to draw around one of the pictures on your stickers canvas. Select *Copy* in the *Edit* menu. In your scenery canvas, click the Maximize button and select *Paste* in the *Edit* menu. The sticker will appear on your canvas.

Click on the sticker and drag it where you want it. Then release the mouse button. Once you click anywhere outside the dotted line around your sticker, you won't be able to move it again.

***Move your stickers into position in your scene.***

# All change

You can vary the size of your stickers, as in the picture above, by using the "shrink and grow" technique described on page 73.

To make a sticker point in another direction, draw around it with the Pick tool and select *Flip Horizontal* or *Flip Vertical* in the *Pick* menu.

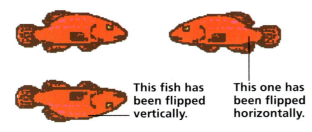

**This fish has been flipped vertically.**

**This one has been flipped horizontally.**

When your clip-art picture is finished, select *Save As...* in the *File* menu, give the file a name, place it in the projects directory and save it.

# More clip-art ideas

You can use clip-art in many different ways. Try producing disguises by adding a selection of hair, glasses and beard stickers to a basic face. Create your own alphabet or design a variety of outfits and accessories to mix and match on a model.

***You can create a rogues gallery of criminals.***

***Design your own alphabet.***

***Design outfits with clip-art.***

# A picture address book

Using an application called Cardfile, you can create an address book to store on your computer. Add cheeky cartoon portraits of your friends to the cards, so that you laugh every time you look at them.

## What is Cardfile?

Cardfile works like a pile of index cards that always remain stacked in alphabetical order. Open Cardfile by double-clicking on its icon in Program Manager.

**This is the Cardfile icon.**

A Cardfile window appears with "(Untitled)" in its Title bar. The window contains one index card, as shown below:

**This is a Cardfile window.**

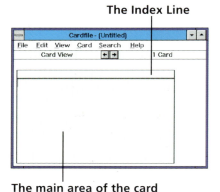

It's a good idea to give your new cardfile a name straight-away. Select *Save As...* in the *File* menu. Give your file a filename with a .CRD extension. Place it in your projects directory and save it.

## Filling the cards

To use the first card that appears when Cardfile opens, double-click in the Index Line area. An Index dialog box opens.

**An Index dialog box**

Type the name of one of your friends in the *Index Line* box. Put their surname first, because address books are usually arranged in alphabetical order according to surname. Then click *OK*.

To add an address and a telephone number, click in the main area of the card. A flashing cursor will appear and you can start typing.

## Adding cards

To add a new card for each of your friends, press the F7 key. In the Index dialog box, type in another friend's name and click *OK*. A new card will appear at the top of your pile.

## Face facts

Pictures added to the index cards will make your address book more colourful. Alternatively, you could add a map showing you how to find a friend's house.

You can draw pictures using Paintbrush and then paste them onto your address cards using the technique below.

## Sizing

To prepare a canvas that is the correct size for your picture, minimize the Cardfile window. Open a copy of Paintbrush by double-clicking on its icon. In the *Options* menu select *Image Attributes...*

In the dialog box that appears, make sure that you are working in centimetres by selecting cm in the *Units* section. Enter a size of about 6cm in the width box and 6cm in the height box. Then click *OK* and close that copy of Paintbrush by double-clicking in its control-menu box.

## Creating a picture

Return to your Cardfile window by double-clicking on its icon at the foot of your screen. Choose the card of one of your friends. Bring it to the front of the pile by clicking on its Index Line. You can also use the arrows below the Cardfile Menu bar to flick through your cards. This is what the arrows look like.

To add a picture to the card, open the *Edit* menu and select *Picture*. Now, click on *Insert Object...* in the *Edit* menu and a dialog box similar to the one below will appear.

***An Insert New Object dialog box***

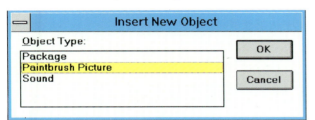

Select *Paintbrush Picture* in the *Object Type* list. When you click *OK,* a Paintbrush window will open containing a correctly sized canvas. Now you are ready to draw a picture.

***A cartoon picture on a canvas in Paintbrush***

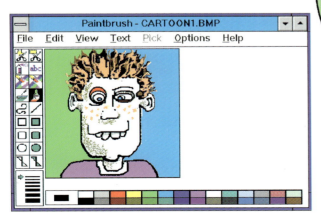

## Inserting a picture

When you have completed your picture, select *Update* in Paintbrush's *File* menu. Then click on *Exit & Return to...* in the *File* menu. The picture will appear on your index card. Drag it into position.

***Each card can have an address and a picture.***

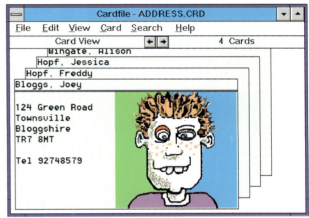

## All change

It's easy to alter an index card if one of your friends moves home or even grows a beard. To change text, select *Text* in Cardfile's *Edit* menu. Alter the name at the top of a card by double-clicking in the Index Line area. A dialog box appears. Make your changes and click *OK*. To alter an address, click in the main area of the card and type in your changes.

To change a picture, select *Picture* in the *Edit* menu. Double-click on the picture you want to alter and a copy of Paintbrush will open. When you have made your alterations, click on *Update* in the *File* menu. Finally, click on *Exit and Return to...* in the *File* menu.

Whenever you add a new card to your cardfile or change an existing card, save the cardfile before closing it. To do this, select *Save* in the *File* menu.

# Character maps and codes

You can use your computer to send baffling, coded messages. People won't be able to understand these messages until you explain how to decode them using an application called Character Map.

## What is a character?

Any letter, number or symbol that your computer can produce is called a character. Each font (see page 60) has up to 256 different characters. This book is printed in a font called Frutiger 45. So, 3, m, @ and # are all characters in that particular font.

## Character Maps

This is the icon for the Character Map application. When you open it, by double-clicking on the icon in Program Manager, a window like the one below appears. It contains a map of all the characters available in one of the fonts stored on your computer.

There are different maps for each of the fonts. To look at the different maps, open the *Font* list and highlight the name of another font. The character map will change to show all the characters available in that particular font.

*This is the Character Map window showing the map of a font called Times.*

This is the name of the font to which all the characters in this map belong.

In this window appears a list of any characters you select.

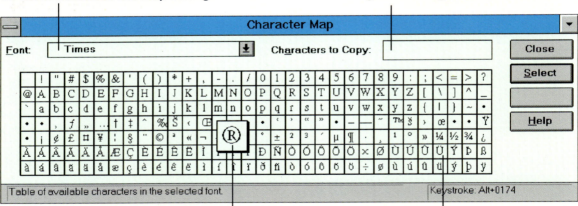

**This character has been magnified using the pointer.**

**Each square contains a different character.**

## A closer look

The character map squares are very small and it can be difficult to see the exact shape of some of the characters. To take a closer look at any character in the map, click on its square and hold down your mouse button. As you click, the square will appear magnified.

80

## Coded messages

To write a coded message, open a copy of Write by double-clicking on its icon in Program Manager. In the *Character* menu select *Fonts...* Select the font called Arial and click *OK*.

Now type into your Write document the secret message you want to send.

Use the cursor to highlight your message. Select *Fonts...* in the *Character* menu again and choose the font called Symbol. Symbol has lots of strange characters.

*This is a coded message in Symbol. Find out how to decode it below.*

Αγεντ Τινκερβελλ
Χομε ανδ φινδ με
ουτσιδε Πηαραοη
Τυτ σ πψραμιδ ατ
μιδνιγητ τονιγητ.
Ι ωιλλ βε δισγυισεδ
ας α χαμελ οωνερ.
Τηε πασσωορδ ισ
Οκλαηομα.
Σιγνεδ

Αγεντ Οβϖιους

To make sure that your message is large enough to read easily when it is printed out, select 14 in the *Size* list in the Fonts dialog box.

Now choose *OK* and your message will be instantly transformed into a mysterious collection of symbols.

## Sending your message

To save your message, select *Save As...* in the *File* menu. Give your file a name, place it in the projects directory and save it. Print out this file onto a piece of paper and send it to a friend. Close the Write window by double-clicking in its control-menu box.

Remember, your friend must have a computer that has Windows software installed, in order to translate your message.

## Tell your friend

Let your friend try and puzzle out the code for a while, but then reveal some clues about how to decode it.

Say that your message is written in Symbol and that using the Character Map application is the only way to decipher it.

## Time to decode

This is what your friend needs to do to decode the message. Open Character Map and select Symbol in the *Font* list. Starting with the first character in your message, use the pointer to move around the map, looking for a character that exactly matches the one in your message.

When your friend finds the right character, he or she should double-click on the square in which the character appears. The symbol will appear in the *Character to Copy* box, like the one below.

Characters to Copy:   Αγεντ Οβϖιους

Your friend should work through in this way, not forgetting to put in spaces where they appear in your message.

## All is revealed

At the end of the message, your friend should click the *Copy* button. Close Character Map by double-clicking in its control-menu box and open a copy of Write. Select *Fonts...* in the *Character* menu. In the *Font* list select the font called Arial and click *OK*. Finally, open Write's *Edit* menu and select *Paste*.

Your message will appear in the Write document decoded and ready to read.

# Invent your own quiz game

You can create a Cardfile with quiz questions on each index card. Using an application called Object Packager, you can hide the answers on the cards. When you want to reveal an answer, all you have to do is double-click.

**A quiz question on an index card**

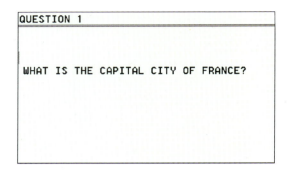

## What is Object Packager?

This is the icon for Object Packager. This application "packages" up one file and inserts it into another. The file that is packaged up is called the object. It can be any kind of file, like a Paintbrush picture or a Write document. The file into which the object is inserted is called the destination file.

The object file appears in the destination file as an icon. When you double-click on this icon the object file automatically opens.

## Questions and answers

To produce a quiz game, start by thinking up a selection of questions and answers. Following the instructions on page 78, create a Cardfile, give it a filename, place it in your projects directory and save it.

Open Cardfile's *Edit* menu and click on *Text*. On your first index card, type a number on the Index Line and a question on the main area of the card. Then minimize Cardfile.

Open a copy of Write and type in the answer to your question. Select *Save As...* in the *File* menu. Give your file a filename (answer1.wri for example), place it in your projects directory and save it.

## Packaging an object

Now you need to package up the answer document and insert it into your index card. Open Object Packager by double-clicking on its icon in Program Manager. In the window, click on the word Content. Select *Import...* in the *File* menu. In the dialog box that opens, highlight answer1.wri in your projects directory and click *OK*.

The filename appears in the Content section of Object Packager's window and a Write icon appears in the Appearance section. Select *Copy Package* in the *Edit* menu and then close Object Packager by double-clicking in its control-menu box.

**This is Object Packager's window containing a packaged Write file.**

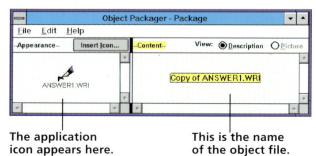

**The application icon appears here.**

**This is the name of the object file.**

82

## Inserting an object

To insert an answer document into an index card, first maximize the Cardfile window. Open the *Edit* menu, select *Picture* so that a tick mark appears beside it. Select *Paste* in the *Edit* menu. A Write icon appears. Drag it into position.

To find out the answer to the question on the card, double-click on this icon. The Write document containing the answer opens. Close it when you have finished by double-clicking in its control-menu box. Repeat this process to add more question cards and answers to your cardfile.

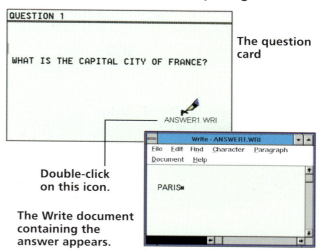

*An index card with a Write file packaged in it*

The question card

Double-click on this icon.

The Write document containing the answer appears.

## Computer sound

Many computers can make sounds. Find out if your computer can by opening Control Panel. Double-click on the Sound icon.

 *This is the Sound icon.*

In the dialog box that opens, there is a list of sound files. They have the filename extension .WAV.

If the files listed in the *Files* section appear dimmed (pale grey), it means that your computer can't make sounds. If they aren't dimmed, highlight one of them and click the *Test* button. You should hear a sound. If you do, you can use some of these sound files in your quiz game.

**The Sound window with a list of .WAV files**

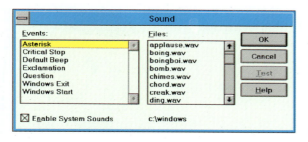

## Adding sounds

Open Object Packager and select *Import...* in the *File* menu. In the dialog box that appears, select the directory called windows. In the *File Name* box, type *.WAV and press the Return key. A list of the .WAV files on your computer appears. You may have one called applause.wav. Highlight it in the *File Name* list, then click OK. If you don't have this file, choose another one. Finally, select *Copy Package* in the *Edit* menu.

Close Object Packager and open your cardfile. Double-click on the Write icon on one of your cards to open an answer file. When it appears, position your cursor at the end of the text and select *Paste* in the *Edit* menu. A Sound icon will appear. Select *Save* in the *File* menu to ensure that the Sound file is saved in your Write file.

Now, if you get the answer right, double-click on this Sound icon and you will hear a round of applause.

83

# Finding a hidden message

Using Object Packager, you can hide a secret file in an innocent-looking letter. Only your friends will know how to reveal the hidden information.

The picture at the bottom of the letter below looks pretty innocent. But when you double-click on it, a Paintbrush file opens revealing a less flattering portrait.

## Compiling a secret file

Next, open Paintbrush and draw a secret picture. When you have finished, select *Save As...* in the *File* menu. Give your file a name (say, secret.bmp), place it in your projects directory and save it. Close Paintbrush by double-clicking in its control-menu box.

## Packaging secrets

Open Object Packager and click on the Content section. Select *Import...* in the *File* menu. In the dialog box that appears, highlight the secret information file (secret.bmp) in your projects directory. When you click OK, the filename will appear in the Content section and a Paintbrush icon in the Appearance section.

## Creating a disguise

Next, you need to disguise the icon in which your secret document is packaged. Click on the Object Packager's Appearance section and select *Cut* in the *Edit* menu. Minimize Object Packager and open a new copy of Paintbrush. Select *Paste* in the *Edit* menu. The icon from the Appearance section will appear on your canvas. Use the Eraser tool to rub it out.

In its place, draw an innocent-looking picture that will fit on your letter. Then, using the Scissor tool, cut around it. Select *Copy* in the *Edit* menu.

Close Paintbrush by double-clicking in its control-menu box. You don't need to save this file.

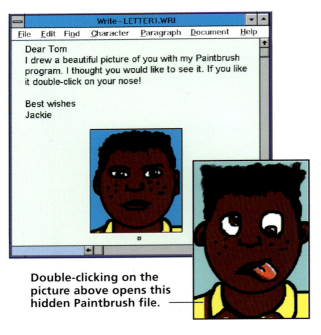

**Double-clicking on the picture above opens this hidden Paintbrush file.**

## An innocent letter

First, you need to create a letter in which to hide a secret file. Open Write by double-clicking on its icon in Program Manager. In the Write window, type a letter. When you have finished, minimize the Write window so that it appears as an icon at the bottom of your screen.

## Hiding the evidence

Maximize Object Packager, and select *Paste* in the *Edit* menu. Your secret picture will appear in the Appearance section. Select *Copy Pac<u>k</u>age* in the *Edit* menu and close Object Packager by double-clicking in its control-menu box.

**The Paintbrush icon is replaced by your picture in Object Packager.**

Maximize the Write file containing your letter. Place your cursor at the bottom of the text. Then select *Paste* in the *Edit* menu and the picture will appear.

To save the letter and the hidden file, select *Save <u>A</u>s...* in Write's *File* menu. Give your file a name (say letter1.wri), place it in your projects directory and save it.

## All is revealed

To reveal the hidden file, all you need to do is double-click on the picture at the bottom of your letter. The Paintbrush file containing your secret picture will open automatically. To close it, double-click in its control-menu box.

## Sending your letter

To send this letter to a friend, copy the letter1.wri file onto a floppy disk. To do this, put a floppy disk in your computer's floppy disk drive. Open File Manager, which has an icon like this. Close all but one of the windows inside the File Manager window. Select *Select Drive...* in the *Disk* menu and in the dialog box that appears select the hard disk drive (usually labelled as the C drive).

A list of the directories on your hard disk will appear in the left-hand side of the window. Find your projects directory and double-click on it.

A list will appear in the right-hand side of the window. Click on your letter1.wri and drag it over to the symbol in the top left-hand corner of the window that looks like this.

This is your floppy disk drive. Release the mouse button. To check that your file has been copied onto the floppy disk, click your pointer on this symbol once. The name of your file will appear in the right-hand side of the window.

## Who does this belong to?

You could set up a picture like the one below. Each character has a picture hidden in it. When you double-click on each character, you can find out who the tutu belongs to.

**Double-click here**     **Double-click here**

**Unlikely!**     **That's more like it.**

85

# Interactive storytime

Most stories have a beginning, a middle, and an end. Their plots never change. But with an "interactive" story, you can decide what happens next by making a series of choices. An interactive story has several possible plots and endings. Using Cardfile, you can write a story that will be different every time you read it.

Make sure that *Picture* is selected in the *Edit* menu and then select *Paste* in the *Edit* menu. When your picture appears, drag it to position.

## Planning your story

To get an idea of how an interactive story works, look at the example on page 87. You need to create a series of index cards, each containing an event and two possible courses of action. Depending on which course you choose, you are directed to another numbered card, where the story continues. By making choices in this way, the plot develops.

Interactive stories are quite difficult to write, so plan your story first. You can make it as complex as you like, with as many cards and choices as you like. Make sure, however, that you include a selection of cards with different endings to your story.

## Adding sounds

If your computer can make sounds you can use Object Packager to add sound files to your index cards. Find out how to check whether your computer can make sounds on page 83. If it can, follow the technique described on page 83 to add sounds to your index cards.

Look at the example interactive story shown on page 87 to see some of the ways in which you can use sounds in a story.

## Jumping between cards

## Creating a story cardfile

To find out how to create a cardfile, look at page 78. Give each index card a number on its Index Line and add the events and choices in your story to the main area of the card.

You can add pictures to some of your cards if you like. To do this, open a copy of Paintbrush. Draw a picture and select the Pick tool to cut it out.

Select *Cut* in the *Edit* menu, and then close Paintbrush without saving the file. Open your Cardfile and click on the card that you want to paste your picture onto.

To move from one card to another, click on the Index Line of the card you want. Alternatively, press the F4 key on the top row of your keyboard. A dialog box appears. Type in the number of the card you require and click OK. That card will jump to the top of your pile.

***This is the Go To dialog box.***

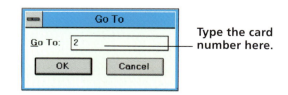

Type the card number here.

## Playing the game

When you are ready to read your story, make sure *Picture* has a tick beside it in Cardfile's *Edit* menu. This will ensure that when you double-click on a Sound icon on a card you will be able to hear the sound file play.

The story below is short and simple. You could set up an identical cardfile to give yourself an idea of how an interactive story works.

When you have written your own interactive story get people to read it. Watch them make choices. Were they the same as yours? They could even write some new index cards themselves to add a whole set of new adventures to the story.

*These are some index cards that make up an interactive story.*

---

**1**

A huge shark has torn a hole in the bottom of your boat. It is sinking fast and you are trapped in a cabin below the deck.

What do you want to do now?
Go to card 2 to try and force open the jammed cabin door.
Go to card 3 to swim out of the hole made by the shark.

---

**2**

When you eventually manage to open the cabin door, a rush of sea water pours in, sweeping you back into the cabin.

What do you want to do now?
Go to card 3 to swim out through the hole made by the shark.
Go to card 4 to cling onto a table in the cabin.

---

**3**

As you swim out of the hole, the shark is waiting to attack you. It swims towards you menacingly.

What do you want to do now?
Go to card 5 to try and reach the lifeboat before the shark bites you.
Go to card 6 to stay and fight off the shark.

---

**4**

The engine room fills with water and the engine explodes. The blast throws you far away from the boat, but near to the shark.

What do you want to do now?
Go to card 5 to swim back toward the lifeboat.
Go to card 6 to swim toward land.

---

**5**

You manage to reach the lifeboat before the shark attacks. With difficulty, you haul yourself safely on board. Only a couple of hours later, a rescue helicopter comes searching for you. You are winched aboard and flown home. When the newspapers hear your story, they buy it for £1000.

---

**6**

The shark swims away and you are able to swim to an island safely. You camp on a beach, waiting to be rescued; but it is six months before anyone finds you. When you finally get home, the newspapers hear of your adventure and pay you £100,000 for the story.

# Macro magic

You can use an application called Recorder to record yourself drawing a picture in Paintbrush. Then watch as the picture magically redraws itself when you play back the recording. Recorder is a difficult application to use, so follow the instructions for this project carefully.

## What is Recorder?

Recorder records the movements of your mouse and any keys that you press. It then plays back these actions. A recorded set of mouse movements and keystrokes is called a macro.

**This is the icon for Recorder.**

You can use Recorder like a video recorder. By recording the way in which a picture is drawn, Recorder can redraw the picture by playing back the recorded actions.

## Preparations

To record yourself drawing a picture, open Paintbrush by double-clicking on its icon in Program Manager. Size the Paintbrush window to fill the top three-quarters of your screen. Select the Brush tool in the Toolbox. Make sure that the background colour selected is white and the foreground colour is black. Finally, minimize Paintbrush.

## Using Recorder

In Program Manager, find the Recorder icon and double-click on it. When the Recorder window opens, select *Record...* in the *Macro* menu. In the dialog box that appears, make the same selections as shown in the following sample Record Macro dialog box.

***A Record Macro dialog box***

**Give your macro a name here.**  **No cross in the *Continuous Loop* check box.**  **In the *Playback* section select *Fast*.**

**Leave this section blank.**  **In the *Record Mouse* section select *Everything*.**  **In the *Relative to* menu select *Window*.**

## Recording a macro

When you have entered these preferences, click the *Start* button. A flashing Recorder icon will appear at the bottom of your screen. This tells you that Recorder is recording. Double-click on the Paintbrush icon at the bottom of your screen and start to draw your picture.

***Simple patterns can look very effective.***

## Stop recording

To stop your recording when you have finished your picture, click once on the Recorder icon at the foot of your screen.

A Recorder dialog box will appear like the one below. Select *Save Macro* and then click *OK*.

**This is the Recorder dialog box.**

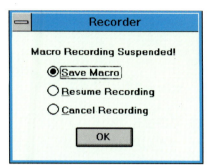

## Preparing for playback

Recorder records the exact position of your pointer on screen. So before you play back a macro, make sure that all the objects on your screen are in the same position as they were before the macro was recorded. If you record a macro and then move, re-size or close windows, it won't play back.

In Paintbrush, make sure that the Brush tool is highlighted and that the background selected colour is white and the foreground colour is black.

Select *New...* in Paintbrush's *File* menu. A dialog box will appear asking "Do you want to save current changes?". Choose *No*. When a new canvas appears, minimize the Paintbrush window.

## Playing a macro

To play back your macro, double-click on the Recorder icon. In the Recorder box, highlight the name of your macro and select *Run* in the *Macro* menu. Watch while your picture redraws itself.

## Speed

You can play back a macro at two different speeds: fast or at the speed at which you recorded it.

To alter the speed, you have to change the selection in the *Playback* section of the Record Marco box before you record a new macro.

## Saving macros

When you have recorded some macros, you can save them all in one file. Select *Save As...* in Recorder's *File* menu. Give your file a filename and a .REC extension. Finally, place it in the projects directory and save it.

## Guessing games

There are lots of ways to use Recorder. Try playing the game below. In Recorder, select *Record...* in the *Macro* menu. In the dialog box, choose *Recorded Speed* in the *Playback* section.

Record a macro of drawing a picture. When you play it back, get your friends to try to guess what the picture is before it is complete.

**A picture is revealed.**

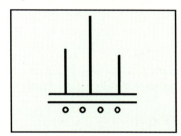

**Can you guess what it is?**

**Now can you guess?**

**So that's what it is!**

# Cartoon fun

Using the Recorder application and a technique called clip-art, you can produce a simple but effective cartoon. This is a difficult project, so don't worry if you take some time to get it right. Follow the stages described below very carefully.

## Scenes and characters

To prepare your cartoon, you need to draw a scene for the action to take place in, and a "character" to move around the scene.

Following the clip-art technique described on pages 76 and 77, open two copies of Paintbrush. Draw a scene on one canvas and a character on the other. Give each picture a different filename (say, scene.bmp and charcter.bmp). Place them both in your projects directory and save them.

**This scenery canvas has an outer space setting with stars and planets.**

**This rocket is the character that will travel through the space scene.**

Maximize the Paintbrush window containing your character. Use the Scissor tool to cut around it. Select *Copy* in the *Edit* menu. Now double-click in the control-menu box to close this window.

## Making preparations

Re-size you scenery canvas to fill the top three-quarters of your screen. Click on its Minimize button, so that it appears as an icon at the foot of your screen. This will ensure that when you restore this Paintbrush window, when you are recording your macro (see page 88), you have plenty of space to work in.

## Setting up your recording

Open Recorder by double-clicking on its icon in Program Manager. Select *Record...* in the *Macro* menu. In the dialog box that appears, make the same selections as in the box shown on page 88. You could, however, select *Recorded Speed* in the *Playback* section, which is a better speed for playing back cartoons.

## Shortcut keys

In the Record Macro dialog box there is a section called *Shortcut Key*. You can choose a code of two keys that, when pressed together, will automatically play back your macro.

If you want to use a shortcut key code, click in the box beside *Enable Shortcut Keys* until a cross appears. In the *Shortcut Key* box select a key from the drop-down list (say, F4). Next, place a cross in one of the boxes beside Ctrl, Shift or Alt (Ctrl, for example). This is your code.

**The Shortcut Key and the Playback sections in the Record Macro dialog box**

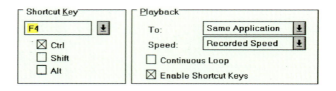

## Recording your cartoon

To start recording your cartoon, click on *Start* in the Record Macro box. Double-click on the Paintbrush logo at the bottom of your screen and your scenery canvas will open.

Select *Paste* in the *File* menu and a copy of your character will appear in your scene. Drag it around your scene, to give the impression of the character moving.

You can move other characters in your scene. Cut them out and drag them. Be careful that you don't cut out part of the background too, or this will move around with your character.

Click on the Recorder icon at the bottom of your screen. The Recorder dialog box will appear. If you want to stop your recording completely, select *Save Macro* and click *OK*.

## Resuming your recording

If you don't want to stop recording, but you want to have time to think about where to move a character next, you can just pause your recording. To do this, click on the Recorder icon.

When you are ready to continue recording, select *Resume Recording* in the Recorder dialog box and then click *OK*.

### The Recorder dialog box

*Resume Recording* is selected.

## Preparing for playback

Remember, before you play back your macro you must put everything back into the position it was in when you started recording.

Select *Open...* in the *File* menu of your scenery Paintbrush window. A box will appear asking you "Do you want to save current changes?". Select *No*. An Open dialog box appears. Highlight the name of your scenery file (scene.bmp) in the *File Name* menu and then click *OK*. Your scenery canvas will re-open, looking as it did before you started recording.

Make sure that the Brush tool is selected and that the foreground colour is black and the background colour is white. Finally, minimize your Paintbrush window.

## A cartoon masterpiece

To play back your cartoon, hold down your two shortcut keys.

The following screens show another idea for a cartoon sequence:

**Cut around the bee with the Scissor tool and drag it around.**

**Make the bee bob from flower to flower.**

**Leave the bee, paste in a butterfly and float it around the flowers.**

# More Windows 3.1 words

The list below explains some of the unusual words that you will come across when tackling the projects in this section of the book. Words in *italics* are explained elsewhere in the list on this page.

If you come across any other unfamiliar words, try looking them up on page 46 or use the Glossary included in the Windows Help system.
You can find out how to use the Glossary on page 45.

**Application**   A computer program that includes the instructions and information that your computer needs to play a particular role, such as word processing or drawing pictures.

**Cardfile**   The Windows *application* that enables you to create a stack of record cards, which are permanently kept in alphabetical order.

**Character Map**   An *application* that shows you a grid containing a picture of the all the letters, numbers and symbols available in a particular *font*.

**Color**   The program that allows you to alter the colours of your Windows display.

**Control Panel**   The Windows *application* that allows you to make changes to the way in which your computer is set up.

**Desktop**   The background area on your screen on which windows appear.

**Directories**   The groups in which files are organized and stored.

**Display**   The *desktop*, windows and icons that you see on your screen.

**Font**   A set of letters, numbers or symbols which have a unique shape and appearance.

**Highlighted text**   Text which has been selected, usually by dragging a cursor over it. It appears with a block around it like `this`.

**Macro**   A series of keystrokes and mouse movements that have been recorded using the *Recorder* program.

**Object Packager**   The Windows *application* that enables you to insert a package of information, such as a picture or a text document, into a window.

**Paintbrush**   The Windows 3.1 *application* that lets you create pictures on your screen.

**Password**   A secret word which gives you access to information. A password can be used to "lock" a *screen saver* on your screen.

**Playback**   When a series of keystrokes or mouse movements that have been recorded are repeated.

**Recorder**   An *application* which allows you to record a series of keystrokes and mouse movements. It can then play them back.

**Screen saver**   A program which replaces the image on your screen with a moving picture.

**Setup box**   A dialog box in which you can specify the way in which you want a program, such as a *screen saver*, to function.

**Shortcut keys**   A code of keystrokes that enable you to select items without using your mouse.

**Software**   A collection of information and instructions that tell your computer exactly how to perform a task.

**Text styles**   The appearance of the letters, numbers and symbols used in a text document. The styles include **bold**, *italic,* underlined and normal text.

**Toolbox**   The part of *a Paintbrush* window which contains the buttons you can use to select different painting effects.

**Wallpaper**   The patterned layer covering the *desktop* of the Windows *display*.

**Write**   This is the word processing *application* in Windows 3.1. It enables you to work with text, changing its shape, size, appearance and position.

# WINDOWS® 95 FOR BEGINNERS

## Gillian Doherty
### Edited by Philippa Wingate

Designed by Russell Punter and Neil Francis
Illustrated by Bill Greenhead
Photography by Howard Allman

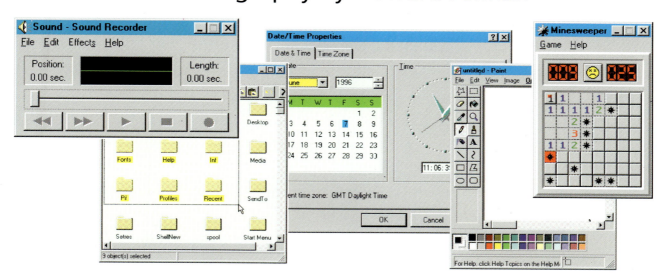

Technical consultant: Nigel Peet
Series editor: Jane Chisholm

# Contents

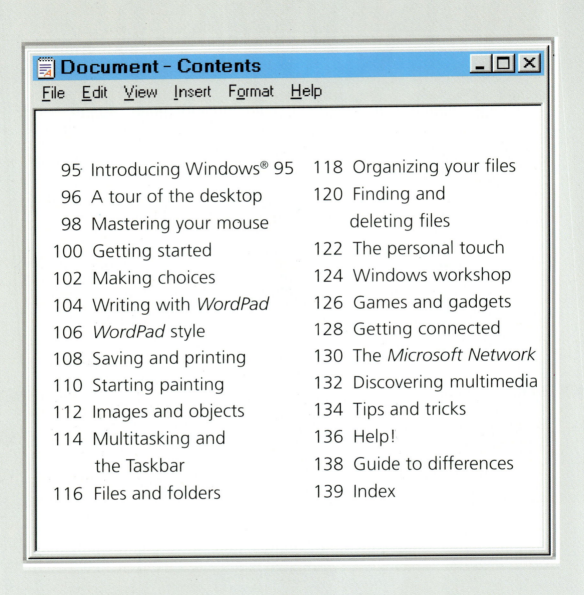

**Document - Contents**

File  Edit  View  Insert  Format  Help

95  Introducing Windows® 95
96  A tour of the desktop
98  Mastering your mouse
100 Getting started
102 Making choices
104 Writing with *WordPad*
106 *WordPad* style
108 Saving and printing
110 Starting painting
112 Images and objects
114 Multitasking and the Taskbar
116 Files and folders
118 Organizing your files
120 Finding and deleting files
122 The personal touch
124 Windows workshop
126 Games and gadgets
128 Getting connected
130 The *Microsoft Network*
132 Discovering multimedia
134 Tips and tricks
136 Help!
138 Guide to differences
139 Index

# Introducing Windows® 95

This section of the book will provide you with all the information you need to get started with Microsoft® Windows® 95. You can find out how to use the programs supplied with Windows 95.

## What is Windows?

Windows 95 is a special kind of program called an operating system. An operating system controls your computer. It enables you to use other programs and tell your computer what to do.

With Windows, you work with pictures, called graphics. You can use these to give the computer instructions.

## What's new in 95?

Windows 95 is the latest version of Windows. The previous versions include Windows 3.1 (see page 1-46), Windows 3.11 and Windows for Workgroups. The new features and improvements are intended to make using your computer easier than ever.

If you already have Windows on your computer, you only need to buy the Windows 95 Upgrade pack. When you put this on your computer, it is added over your existing version of Windows. This means that you keep any programs that are already on your computer. The way that your programs are organized will also stay the same, making it easy for you to find things.

There is a section on page 136 for anybody who has used a previous version of Windows. This guides you through some of the main differences with Windows 95 and helps you to look up the new ways of carrying out certain tasks.

**Windows 95 Upgrade**

## What do you need?

For most of the things you will do in this section, all you need is the Windows 95 software.

We have assumed that you already have Windows 95 on your computer. If you don't, you will need to put it on, called installing it. When you buy Windows 95, it comes with instructions telling you how to do this.

## What next?

If you are just starting to use Windows 95, you should work your way through this section of the book from the beginning and follow what is happening on your computer at the same time. This will help you to become familiar with the basics of Windows 95.

If you want to know how to do something specific, turn to the index at the end of the book to see where you can find out about it.

## Solving problems

If you get stuck, Windows 95 has its own help system. Turn to page 136 to find out how to use it.

Throughout this section there are warning boxes containing the symbol shown below. These are to alert you to problems that you might come across and give you hints for avoiding or solving them.

**Warning symbol**

95

# A tour of the desktop

This section tells you how to start Windows 95 and guides you through some of the first things you'll see on your screen. You'll also receive a tour of the Windows 95 desktop and find out about the items on it.

## Ready, steady, go

Windows 95 starts automatically when you switch on your computer. After a few seconds, the message **Starting Windows 95** will appear.

It takes Windows 95 about a minute to start up. During this time, you may see several pages of text flash onto your screen. You will also see a picture of a tiny egg-timer. This means that Windows 95 is busy starting up. While you are waiting, a screen like the one below will be displayed.

**The Windows 95 opening screen**

## The desktop

After the opening screen of Windows 95, a coloured or patterned display called the desktop will appear. It contains several small pictures, called icons, which each represent a particular program.

The desktop is the area where you use the programs on your computer. Like a real desk, the Windows 95 desktop is a workspace containing lots of different tools to help you work.

The picture below shows some of the things you can expect to find on your desktop. Don't worry if it doesn't show the same icons as this one; some computers have different programs.

### My Computer
This icon allows you to look at what information is stored on your computer. Find out about it on page 116.

### Recycle Bin
When you no longer need a document, you can throw it into the *Recycle Bin*. Find out how to use it on page 120.

### My Briefcase
If you sometimes work on different computers, this program helps you to keep them up-to-date. Find out how to use it on page 128.

### Network Neighborhood
This program will help you if your computer is connected to other computers. Find out about it on page 129.

### The Microsoft Network
This icon enables you to connect your computer to Microsoft's information service. Find out more about it on page 130.

### Inbox
This program enables you to create, send, and receive electronic mail. Find out more about it on page 131.

### Start button
The Start button provides you with access to almost everything you need to use in Windows 95. Find out about it on page 100.

### Warning!
When you have finished using your computer, you must tell it to shut down before you turn it off. Find out how to do this on page 125.

### Desktop
This is the desktop itself. Your desktop may have a different patterned or coloured layer.

### Welcome box
The Welcome box may appear on your desktop. Each time you switch on, it gives you a different tip.

### Taskbar
When you start using programs, the Taskbar will contain buttons for each program that is being used. Find out more about it on page 114.

### Windows tour
Why not take Windows 95's own tour? It shows you some basic skills and gives you an opportunity to try them out for yourself. Turn to page 137 to find out how to start it.

# Mastering your mouse

One of the most important tools you will need to use Windows 95 effectively is a mouse. Windows 95 uses pictures to present information and you give your computer instructions by "touching" these pictures using a mouse.

On these pages, you'll find out about the different ways in which you can use a mouse to make things happen.

**This device is called a mouse because of its shape and long tail-like cable.**

## Moving your mouse

When you move your mouse around on a flat surface, it sends signals to a pointer on the screen. This pointer follows the movements of your mouse.

Try pointing at the different icons on the desktop by moving the mouse until the tip of the pointer is positioned over an icon.

**Pointing at an icon**

Some computers have a device called a touchpad instead of a mouse. You use a touchpad by moving your finger across its surface.

*A computer with touchpad*

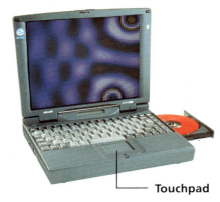

Touchpad

## Pointer power

The main pointer symbol you'll come across is this simple arrow.

 **Arrow pointer**

As you move the pointer around the display, you will notice that it sometimes changes shape. It changes according to the tasks for which you can use it. Here are some of the different shaped pointers you may see.

**Pointer symbols**

## Mouse buttons

In order to touch the items on your display, you need to press the buttons on your mouse. There are two main ways of touching things: clicking and double-clicking.

Throughout this book, whenever you are told to click on something, you should use the left mouse button, unless the right mouse button is specified. The picture below shows which mouse button is which. If a mouse has more than two buttons, it is the outer buttons that are important.

*A mouse*

Right button

Left button

## Clicking

You can touch, or click on, icons and certain parts of your display by pointing at them and pressing and releasing a mouse button. Clicking on items in this way gives your computer information.

Try clicking once on the *My Computer* icon. The icon will change colour. You have now selected it. This means that you have told the computer that you want to do something to the icon. To deselect the icon, click on a blank part of the desktop.

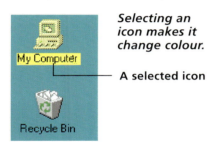

*Selecting an icon makes it change colour.*

— A selected icon

If you still have a Welcome box on your desktop (see page 97), you can close it by clicking once on the cross in the top right-hand corner of the box.

## Double-clicking

Double-clicking means pressing a mouse button twice very quickly. It usually offers a shortcut to carrying out a particular task.

Try double-clicking on the *My Computer* icon. A box containing several icons will appear on your desktop. Close it by clicking once on the cross in the top right-hand corner.

Close button

## The right button

The right mouse button also allows you to take shortcuts.

Try clicking on the *My Computer* icon with the right mouse button. A list like the one below will appear. Click on a blank part of the desktop to make the list disappear.

*Clicking with the right mouse button opens a list like this one.*

You'll find out more about what the right button allows you to do later in the book.

## Dragging

To move things around on your desktop you need to use a technique called dragging. Try pointing at the *My Computer* icon again. Press and hold down the left mouse button. Keeping the button pressed, move your mouse. The icon on the screen will move too.

When you have finished dragging an object, release the mouse button to drop it.

Now try dragging an icon with the right mouse button pressed instead of the left button. When you release it, a menu will appear. To get rid of the menu, click on the desktop with the left button.

*Dragging an icon*

## Mouse trouble

Are you left-handed? Your mouse is probably prepared for a right-handed user, which means that you may find it a little awkward to use. To find out how to make it suitable for a left-handed user, see page 134.

Beware! The instructions in this book are for a right-handed mouse. If you do change the way your mouse works, your left and right mouse buttons will swap roles.

# Getting started

The Start button is the place where you will begin most of the things you want to do in Windows 95. You can use it to start, or launch, a program. Each program appears on your desktop in a box called a window. On these pages you will find out about the main parts of a window.

## Starting up
The Start button is positioned at the end of the Taskbar. If you rest your pointer over it for a few seconds, a message which reads **Click here to begin** will appear.

**The Start button**

Try clicking on the Start button. A list, called a menu, opens. Some of the items on the menu have arrowheads beside them. When you select one of these items, by resting your pointer over it for a second, another menu will open.

*Menus opening out from the Start button*

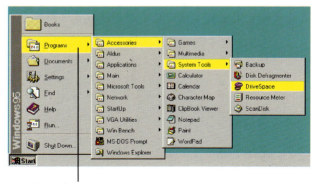

**A selected item**

## Launching a program
Now try launching a program called *WordPad*. To do this, select the word *Programs* from the first menu above the Start button. The menu that opens contains the names of collections of programs, called program groups. *WordPad* is usually in a program group called *Accessories*. To launch the *WordPad* program, simply click on its name. It will appear in a window on your desktop.

## What is a window?
A window is a rectangular space in which you work with a particular program. When a program is running in a window, the window is said to be open.

The screen below shows a typical window and names some of its main parts.

*A WordPad window*

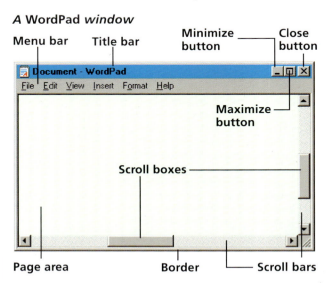

## Maximizing and restoring
To take a closer look at a window, you can enlarge it by clicking on its Maximize button. When a window is maximized, it fills the whole screen so that you can't see its border. Its Maximize button disappears and is replaced by a Restore button. When you click on the Restore button, the window will return to its original size and position on your desktop.

*When a window isn't maximized, you can still see the desktop.*

*A maximized window fills the entire desktop.*

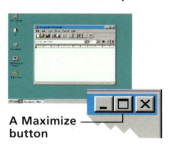

**A Maximize button**

**A Restore button**

## Minimizing

When you are not using a window, you can clear it off your desktop by reducing it to an icon. To do this, click on its Minimize button. This shrinks the window so that it only appears as a button on the Taskbar. The program is still running, but it is tucked out of the way.

When you want to enlarge the window again, click on the button that represents the program on the Taskbar and it will return to its previous size and position.

**A Minimize button**

**A program button**

## Resizing a window

As long as a window hasn't been maximized, you can alter its size and shape. To do this, move the pointer over the border of the window. It will change to a double-headed arrow. If you hold down the left mouse button and drag the border, you can change the height and width of the window. Release the mouse button when the window is the size you want.

*A window can be stretched in different directions.*

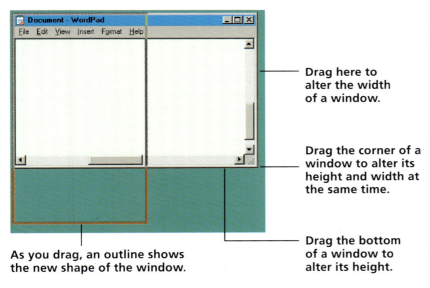

Drag here to alter the width of a window.

Drag the corner of a window to alter its height and width at the same time.

Drag the bottom of a window to alter its height.

As you drag, an outline shows the new shape of the window.

## Moving a window

If a window hasn't been maximized, you can move it around your desktop. To do this, point at a blank part of its Title bar. Holding down the left mouse button, drag the window to a new location. Release the mouse button to drop the window into its new position.

## Scroll bars

The window below has scroll bars along its right and bottom edges. This tells you that it is too small to display all of its contents. Each scroll bar has a scroll box on it. Dragging a scroll box along a scroll bar allows you to look at different parts of the area inside a window. If you only want to move a little at a time, click on the arrowheads at either end of the scroll bar.

*A window with scroll bars*

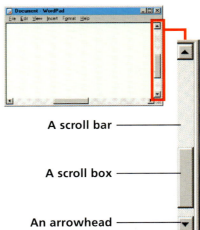

A scroll bar

A scroll box

An arrowhead

## Closing a window

When you have finished using a program, you can stop it running by closing its window. To do this, click on its Close button.

**A Close button**

101

# Making choices

You can give your computer instructions by choosing from certain options inside a window. There are many different ways of doing this. On these pages, you will see some of the main ways.

## Menu bar and menus

When you launch a program, you will see a Menu bar along the top of its window. Look at the *WordPad* window you opened on page 8 to see for yourself.

To open a menu, click on its name on the Menu bar. If you then move the pointer along the Menu bar, this opens the other menus one at a time. To close a menu, click on its name again or press the Esc key on your keyboard.

*Opening a menu*

A menu name

An open menu

## Menu symbols

Some menu options have symbols beside them. The menu below shows what some of these symbols mean.

*Different types of menu symbols*

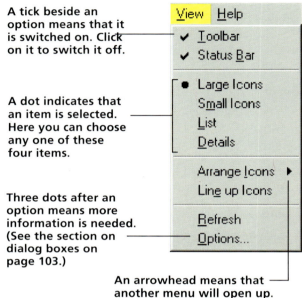

A tick beside an option means that it is switched on. Click on it to switch it off.

A dot indicates that an item is selected. Here you can choose any one of these four items.

Three dots after an option means more information is needed. (See the section on dialog boxes on page 103.)

An arrowhead means that another menu will open up.

## Menu options

A menu contains a list of options. These options represent different kinds of instructions that you can give to your computer. You select an option by clicking on it.

You can use options to tell your computer to carry out certain tasks, such as printing out documents, or to switch on particular features on the display. Sometimes, when you select an option, you will be asked to give more information about your choice before a task can be carried out.

If an option is shown in light grey print, this tells you that it is not available. If you click on one of these options, nothing will happen.

## Keyboard commands

Some menu options have codes, called keyboard commands, beside them. This means that you can tell your computer what to do by simultaneously pressing the keys indicated by the code, instead of selecting the option with your mouse. Using keyboard commands can be a quicker way of giving instructions once you remember which keys to press.

Most keyboard commands include the Control, Alt or Shift keys, followed by a letter. For example, instead of selecting the *Print* option on *WordPad's File* menu, you can press the Control key and the letter P

**Alt key**   **Shift key**   **Control key**

102

## Dialog boxes

If you select a menu option that is followed by three dots, a box, called a dialog box, will open. You use this box to give the computer more information about your choice.

Completing a dialog box is like filling in a questionnaire. You are given several choices and your responses tell the computer exactly what you want to do.

Windows 95 has several different ways of letting you indicate your choices. The picture below shows some of the features you will find in dialog boxes.

## Dividers

Some dialog boxes are divided into different sections called property sheets. Each section is represented by a sheet with a tab at the top. To see an example, open *Control Panel* from the *Settings* menu on the Start menu. Double-click on the *Mouse* icon. The *Mouse Properties* dialog box shown below will appear.

**The Mouse Properties *dialog box***

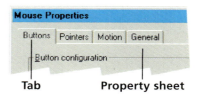

Tab          Property sheet

To look at the contents of a particular sheet, click on the relevant tab. Try looking at the *Pointers* sheet by clicking on its tab. Each sheet is like a separate dialog box.

*An example dialog box*

**A Drop-down list box.** Click on the arrowhead to open a list of options.

**A List box.** Select an option by clicking on its name. Use the scroll bar to see the rest of the list.

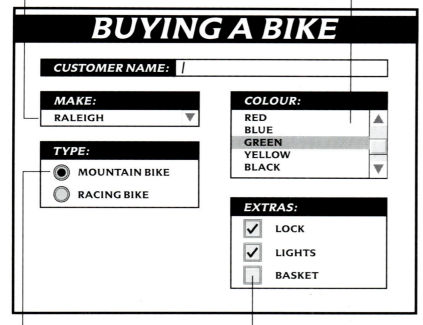

**An Option button.** When you select an option like this, a black dot appears in the button next to it. Clicking on a different option switches the first one off.

**A Check box.** Click in a box to switch an option on or off. When an option is on, a tick appears in the box.

## Command buttons

All dialog boxes contain buttons. Many of them have commands such as *Save* or *Display* written on them. To use a command button, simply click on it.

**A command button**

The most common command buttons you will come across are *OK* and *Cancel* buttons. When you have finished making your selections in a dialog box, you can tell your computer to put the changes into effect by clicking on the *OK* button.

To close a dialog box without making any changes, click on its *Cancel* button.

103

# Writing with *WordPad*

*WordPad* is a program which comes with Windows 95. You can use it to type in and organize text and to change the way the text looks. This is called word processing.

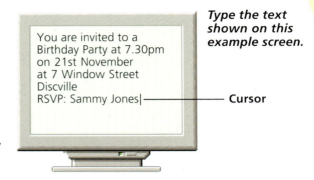

*Type the text shown on this example screen.*

Cursor

## About *WordPad*
Launch *WordPad* from the *Accessories* menu by clicking on its name. Make sure its window is maximized so that you can see it clearly.

*The* WordPad *window*

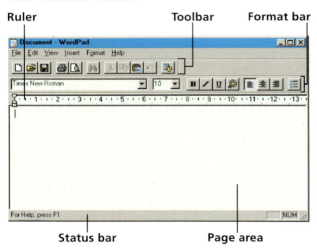

Ruler    Toolbar    Format bar

Status bar    Page area

The *WordPad* window above contains tools to help you to work with a text document. There is a Toolbar, Format bar, Ruler and Status bar. If any of these items is not shown in your *WordPad* window, you can switch it on by clicking on its name on the *View* menu.

## Write on
When you launch *WordPad*, a flashing vertical line, called the cursor, appears in the top left-hand corner of the page area. This shows where text will appear when you start to type.

Try typing the text shown on the following example screen. As you type, the text automatically "wraps" onto the next line when it reaches the end of a line. If you want to make it start a new line yourself, you can do this by pressing the Return (or Enter) key.

## Moving the cursor
When you move the pointer over the page area, it changes into an I-shaped pointer. You can use this to position the cursor. Before you can move it to an area of the page where there is no text, you'll need to use the Return key to move down the page. Then point to where you want the cursor to go and click with the mouse button. It jumps to the point where you clicked. When you start typing, the text will appear at that point.

**I-shaped pointer**

## Selecting text
You can mark a section of text that you want to change by selecting it. To do this, position the pointer to the left of the text you want to select. Holding down the mouse button, drag the pointer to the end of the section. This highlights the text. You can deselect text by clicking elsewhere in the window.

**Selected text**

## ⚠ Warning!
Be careful when you have selected text. Anything that you type will replace the text that is highlighted. If you replace something by mistake, stay calm! Clicking on the Undo button will make your selected text reappear.

**Undo button**

104

> **⚠ Warning!**
> The Clipboard can only store one section of text at a time. As soon as you copy something new, it replaces whatever was on the Clipboard before.

## Deleting text

If you make a mistake when typing in text, you can correct it. Text is made up of letters, numbers and symbols called characters. The Delete key deletes the character to the right of the cursor and the Backspace key deletes the character to the left.

You can delete a whole section of text at once by selecting it and then pressing either the Delete or the Backspace key.

**Backspace key**   **Delete key**

## Cut and paste

You can move sections of text from one part of a document to another. To do this, select the text you want to move and then click on the Cut button shown below. The selected text will disappear from the document. The text is actually moved to a special location called the Clipboard where it is stored.

Now position the cursor where you want to move the text and click on the Paste button. This pastes the text from the Clipboard into your document.

**Cut button**

**Paste button**

## Copying text

You can use the Clipboard to copy text. Select the text you want to copy and then click on the Copy button shown below. The text remains where it is, but a copy of it is sent to the Clipboard. You can paste the copied text into another position in your document by clicking on the Paste button.   **Copy button**

## Finding text

*WordPad* has a feature called *Find* which allows you to search for a particular word in your document. Click on the button shown on the right to open the *Find* dialog box.

**Find button**

Click in the *Find what* box and enter the word you are looking for. Use the check boxes to tell the computer exactly what to search for. Selecting *Match whole word only* tells the computer not to look for the word inside longer words. For example, if the word you typed was "invite", it would not look for words like "invited" and "invites". Selecting *Match case* tells the computer to look only for words that have the same capital and small letters.

Click on the *Find Next* button to start the search. The program searches for the first time the word occurs and highlights it.

**The Find *dialog box***

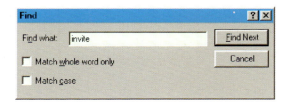

## Replacing text

You can find and replace a particular word by selecting *Replace* from the *Edit* menu. Type the word you are looking for in the *Find what* box. Then type the word with which you want to replace it in the *Replace with* box. Click on the *Replace* button to search for and replace the next matching word, or *Replace All* to replace the word every time it occurs in your document.

# WordPad style

WordPad has lots of tools for improving the way a document looks. You can use these tools to change the shape, position and style of your text.

## Style choices

WordPad offers several different ways of changing the way text looks. You can alter the shape of the characters that make up your text by changing the "font". You can also change the size of the letters and choose from text styles such as underlined, *italic* or **bold**. Before you can change text in your document, you will need to select it (see page 104).

Click on the *Font* option on the *Format* menu to see the fonts and styles that are available. If you click on an option, the sample box shows how your text will look if you select that option. Click on *OK* when you have made your choices.

*The* **Font** *dialog box*

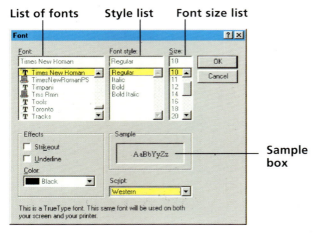

**List of fonts**   **Style list**   **Font size list**

**Sample box**

## The Format bar

The *WordPad* program includes a device called the Format bar. This offers an alternative way of changing the appearance of your text.

When you open *WordPad*, the Format bar should be displayed across the top of the window. If it isn't, turn to page 104 to find out how to switch it on.

## Format buttons

The buttons and boxes on the Format bar offer quick ways of making some of the same changes you can make using the *Font* dialog box. To use one of these buttons, first highlight the text you want to change and then click on the button.

*Use these buttons and boxes to change your text.*

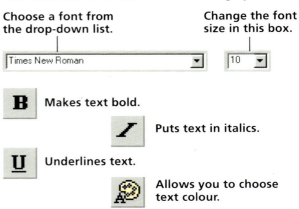

**Choose a font from the drop-down list.**   **Change the font size in this box.**

Makes text bold.

Puts text in italics.

Underlines text.

Allows you to choose text colour.

## Positioning text

The buttons below allow you to change the position of your text on the page. This is called aligning the text. You can line it up with the left or right edge of the page, or position it between the two.

*Buttons for positioning text*

**Lines text up against the left-hand side.**   **Positions text in the middle.**   **Lines text up against the right-hand side.**

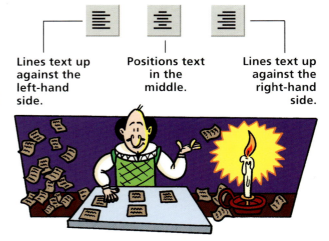

## *Page Setup*

When you create a document in *WordPad*, you need to tell your computer what size page you want and where you want to position the text on the page. To do this, choose *Page Setup* from the *File* menu.

Use the *Size* drop-down list in the *Paper* section to tell the computer what size paper you are using to print out your document.

**The Page Setup *dialog box***

The *Portrait* and *Landscape* options allow you to choose between a vertical and a horizontal page setup.

***These pictures show how the page will look.***

Portrait      Landscape

Use the *Margins* section to tell your computer how much space to leave between the edge of the page and the edge of your text. To do this, simply click in a box and enter a new distance value.

## Using the Ruler

You can use *WordPad*'s Ruler (see page 104) to help you arrange your text on the page.

When you press the Tab key on your keyboard, the cursor jumps a set distance. The Ruler can be used to change this distance. To see how this works, try clicking on the Ruler at several different points. L-shaped symbols, called tab stops, will appear at the points where you clicked.

When you press the Tab key on your keyboard, the cursor jumps so that it is in line with the next tab stop. When you start to type, the text will appear at that point.

You can move a tab stop by dragging it. To get rid of it entirely, drag it beyond the left edge of the Ruler.

***Tab stops can help you to line up text.***

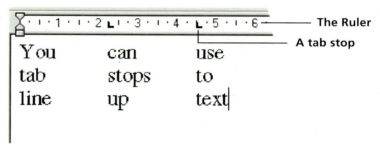

## Be creative

Try using some of the tools and techniques you have read about to alter the invitation you typed on page 104. Here are some suggestions for things to try.

107

# Saving and printing

When you have created a document, Windows 95 allows you to store it. This is called saving a document. You can also print out a copy on paper.

## About disks

The main places you can store documents, or files, are your computer's hard disk and floppy disks. The hard disk is inside the computer and can store lots of information. Floppy disks are made of plastic and can be used to keep copies of your files, or to carry files to another computer.

## The *Save As* box

When you save a file, you need to give it a name and tell your computer where to store it. In Windows 95 programs, you can do this by choosing the *Save As* option from the *File* menu.

If you try saving the *WordPad* document you created on page 107, a dialog box like the one below will appear on your desktop.

*The Save As dialog box*

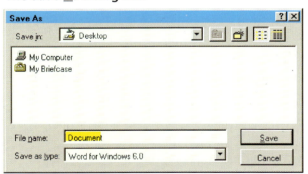

## Naming a file

Click in the *File name* box to enter a name for your file. It can be up to 255 characters long and can include spaces but none of these characters: /\*<>?": |

Always give files descriptive names so that you can remember what they contain. For example, save the *WordPad* document you created on page 107 using the name **WordPad Invitation**.

## Where to save

Open the *Save in* drop down list in the *Save As* box. You use this to tell your computer where to store a file when it saves it. It probably contains icons for your disk drives, *My Briefcase, My Computer* and the desktop. The hard disk drive is normally labelled **C:**. In this book it is referred to as the C drive.

## Saving a file

Now try saving WordPad Invitation. To do this, open the *Save in* drop-down list and click on the C drive icon. In the box below, select the icon with the word Windows beside it and click on the *Open* button. This tells your computer that you want to save WordPad Invitation in a place called the Windows folder on the C drive. This is only for temporary storage. Turn to page 118 to find out about organizing and storing documents.

Now click on the *Save* button. While the computer is saving the file, your pointer will change to an egg-timer. This tells you that the computer is busy carrying out an instruction.

**The "busy" symbol**

## Existing files

If you type a file name that is the same as a file already on the disk, a message appears asking whether you want to replace the existing file with the one you are trying to save. Click on the *Yes* button to replace it, or click on *No* and then choose a different name for the file.

You only need to use the *Save As* command if you are saving a new file. If you have just changed an existing file, you can save it by clicking on the Save button.

**Save button**

# Preparing to print

Before you can print out a file, you need to check that your computer and printer are properly connected and that you have loaded the printer with paper.

Your printer also needs to be switched on and "on-line", which means that it is ready to receive your printing instructions. Most printers have an on-line button with a light beside it to show when the printer is ready.

# Print preview

Check that your document looks the way you want it to before you print it. Click on the Print Preview button to see the whole document at once.

**Print Preview button**

# The *Print* box

You need to give your computer information about the kind of printer you are using and what you want it to print. In Windows 95 programs, you can do this by choosing the *Print* option from the *File* menu. This opens a *Print* dialog box like the one shown below.

In the *Printer* section, select the name of the printer you are using from the *Name* drop-down list.

**The Print *dialog box***

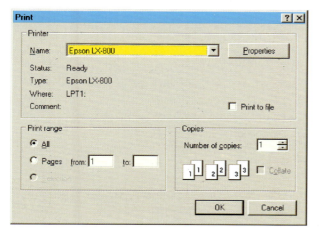

# Which pages?

If a document has several pages, you can choose which ones you want to print in the *Print range* section of the *Print* dialog box. To print all of the pages, select *All*.

# Number of copies

You can choose how many copies of your document you want to print in the *Copies* section of the *Print* dialog box. Click on the arrowheads to change the number of copies.

When you have entered all the print information, click on *OK* to start printing. A message confirming that your document is being printed will appear briefly in a box on your desktop.

# Printing

When a file is being printed, you will see a printer icon at the end of the Taskbar. Double-click on it to open the *Print Manager* window.

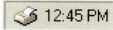

**Printer icon**

Your printer can only print one file at a time. If you try to print a second one, *Print Manager* holds it in a queue until the printer is ready. The *Print Manager* window shows the order in which files will be printed.

To cancel a print command, click on the name of the file you want to cancel with the right mouse button. Then, from the menu that appears, select *Cancel Printing*.

**The Print Manager *window***

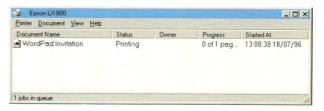

109

# Starting painting

The Windows 95 package contains a program called *Paint*, which you can use to create pictures on your computer screen.

## About *Paint*

*Paint* is usually found in the *Accessories* program group. Click on its name to launch it, and then maximize its window.

The *Paint* window below contains a colour palette and a collection of buttons called the Toolbox. These buttons represent drawing and painting tools.

*The* **Paint** *window*

## Selecting colours

Before you start drawing, you need to select the colours you want to use. Choose a background colour to draw on and a foreground colour to draw with.

To select a foreground colour, click on a colour from the palette with the left mouse button. Use the right mouse button to select a background colour.

## Shape tools

The tools shown below enable you to draw different shapes.

*Shape tools*

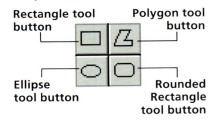

To use a Shape tool, click on its button and move your pointer to where you want the shape to appear on the page. Keeping the left mouse button pressed, drag the mouse to create the shape you want.

You can use the Rectangle and Ellipse tools to create perfect squares and circles by holding down the Shift button while you drag a shape.

The Polygon tool enables you to create a shape with many sides. You use it by dragging out connected lines. Join the end of the last line to the start of the first line to create a closed shape.

When you select a shape tool, you can choose from the different methods of shading shown below.

*Shading options*

**Draws outline of shape in foreground colour, with no shading**

**Draws outline in foreground colour, but shades shape in background colour**

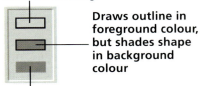

**Draws and shades shape in background colour**

## Painting tools

There are several tools, shown below, that allow you to use different styles of drawing, painting and shading.

To select one of these tools, click on its button. Moving your mouse moves the tool on the screen. To draw with the tool, keep the mouse button pressed while you move the mouse around.

You can shade in a closed shape by selecting the Fill tool and then clicking on the area that you want to shade. This fills the shape with the foreground colour.

*Drawing and painting tools*

 Pencil tool button

 Brush tool button

 Airbrush tool button

 Fill tool button

## Different strokes

You can change the width of the strokes made by some of the tools. If this option is available for a particular tool, when you select that tool a box displaying the different stroke widths will appear below the Toolbox. Click on the width you require.

*Different stroke widths for the Brush tool*

110

## Line tools

The tools shown below allow you to draw straight or curved lines by clicking and dragging.

To create a curved line, select the Curve tool. Hold down the mouse button and drag out a straight line. Then click and drag the line at two points to create curves.

You can use the Line tool to draw a straight line vertically, horizontally, or at a 45° angle, by holding down the Shift key as you drag.

 Line tool button

 Curve tool button

## Text tool

You can add text to a picture using the Text tool. Select the tool and then click at the point where you want to position the text. A box containing a flashing cursor will appear. When you start typing, the text will appear in this box. Drag the border of the box to create more space.

 Text tool button

Use the Text toolbar, shown below, to alter the font, style and size of the text. If you can't see the toolbar, switch it on from the *View* menu.

*Text toolbar*

## Other tools

Other useful tools in the *Paint* Toolbox are the Eraser tool and the Magnifier tool.

If you make a mistake when drawing, drag the Eraser tool over the area you want to erase. It shades over the area with the background colour that is selected.

The Magnifier tool allows you to look at an area in more detail. When you select it, a rectangle will appear. Position it over the area of your picture that you want to magnify and click with the mouse button. This zooms in on the selected area. You can zoom back out by selecting the Magnifier tool again and clicking anywhere on the page.

Eraser tool button

Magnifier tool button

## Practise painting

Try using *Paint* to create a picture to go with the invitation that you created using the *WordPad* program. You can find out how to put the two together on page 112.

*Painting your own picture*

Use the Rectangle tool to create box-shaped presents.

Use the Fill tool to colour in shapes.

The Airbrush tool creates this fuzzy effect.

Use the Polygon tool to create unusual shapes.

### Save it!

Use the Save *As* command to save your picture (see page 108). Name it **My Picture** and save it in the Windows folder.

111

# Images and objects

You can move and copy a section of a picture, called an image, within the *Paint* program using the cut and paste method you used in *WordPad* (see page 105). You can also combine work created in different programs. For example, you can add a picture created in *Paint* to a *WordPad* document. A file added in this way is called an object.

## Selection tools

Before you can move, copy or delete an area of your *Paint* picture, you need to select it. You do this using the tools shown below.

| Rectangle Selection tool | Freeform Selection tool |
|---|---|

To use the Rectangle Selection tool, hold down the mouse button and drag a box around the area of your picture you want to select.

You can use the Freeform Selection tool to select an irregularly shaped area of your picture. Hold down the mouse button and draw around the area you want to select with the solid black line. When you release the mouse button, the shape will change to a dotted rectangle. However, it is still the irregular shape that is selected.

## Moving pictures

To move a selected shape within a *Paint* picture, hold down the left mouse button while you drag it.

You can make a copy of a selected shape by holding down the Ctrl key as well as the mouse button. This leaves the original picture in place, but allows you to move a copy of it.

## Mirror image

The *Image* menu in *Paint* contains options which allow you to turn sections of your picture around, or flip them over.

To use an *Image* command, select the area of the picture you want to alter. Then choose a command from the *Image* menu.

**This picture shows the effects some of the Image commands have.**

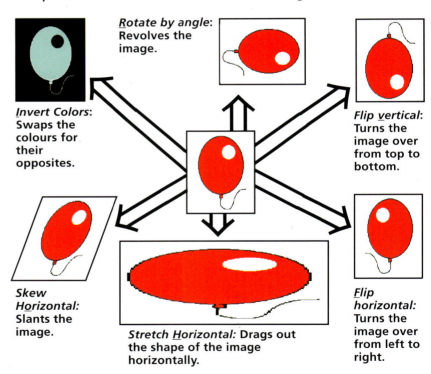

*Invert Colors*: Swaps the colours for their opposites.

*Rotate by angle*: Revolves the image.

*Flip vertical*: Turns the image over from top to bottom.

*Skew Horizontal*: Slants the image.

*Stretch Horizontal*: Drags out the shape of the image horizontally.

*Flip horizontal*: Turns the image over from left to right.

## About objects

You can easily combine work created in different programs by inserting a file created in one program into a file created in a different program. An inserted file is called an object. An object can be text, pictures or even a sound or video file.

Windows 95 offers several different ways of inserting an object into a file.

112

## Pasting between programs

The easiest way of moving sections of pictures or text between files in different programs is by using the *Copy* and *Paste* commands.

Try pasting the picture you created in *Paint* into WordPad Invitation. Open the My Picture file (in the Windows folder on the C drive). Use a selection tool to select the area you want to copy and select *Copy* from the *Edit* menu.

Open WordPad Invitation (in the Windows folder on the C drive). Position the cursor where you want the picture to appear. (It is easiest to paste the picture on a line without any text.) Then select *Paste* from the *Edit* menu.

**You can use this technique to create a striking party invitation.**

## Object embedding

There are certain kinds of objects, such as sounds, that are best inserted into other files using a method called embedding.

To embed an object, open the file into which you want to insert the object. Then select *Object* from the *Insert* menu. In the *Insert Object* dialog box, select the *Create from File* option.

To locate the file you want to insert, click on the *Browse* button. In the *Browse* dialog box that appears, open the *Look in* drop-down list and click on the icon for the drive or folder where the file is stored. When you find the file's name, select it and click on the *Insert* button. This inserts the object into the file.

To make changes to an embedded object, use the same method as for a pasted object.

**The** Insert Object **dialog box**

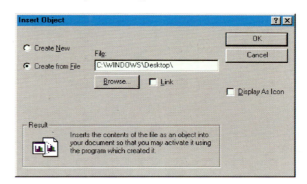

## Working with objects

When you have pasted an object into a file, you can make changes to it by double-clicking on it. For example, double-click on the *Paint* object. A *Paint* window containing the picture will open. Make the alterations you want and then close the *Paint* window. Any changes will be shown on the picture in the *WordPad* document.

If you click on an object just once, a frame with eight handles appears around it. You can resize an object by clicking and dragging its handles. To move a framed object, hold down the mouse button and drag. The pointer changes to a pointer attached to a rectangle. Move it to where you want to position the picture and then release the mouse button.

You can also use the align buttons on the Format bar (see page 106) to position the picture in the middle, left, or right of the page.

**A framed picture**

**A handle**

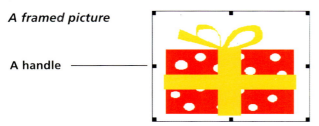

## Object linking

You can use a method called linking to create a connection between an object and the file it came from. This means that whenever you make a change to the file and save it, the object will be changed too.

The link option is useful for objects that need to be updated. For example, you might want to use a table of figures created in *WordPad* in a leaflet created in *Paint*. If the object is linked, changing and saving the figures in one file will also change them in the other.

To link an object, follow the method for embedding an object, but make sure *Link* is selected in the *Insert Object* dialog box.

# Multitasking and the Taskbar

Windows 95 has a feature called multitasking which allows you to do more than one job at the same time. When you are doing several jobs at once, you can use the Taskbar to help you to control the different windows that are open, and to keep your desktop organized.

## The Taskbar
The main use of the Taskbar is to help you keep track of which programs are open on your desktop. Each program is represented by a button on the Taskbar, as shown on the big Taskbar running across the bottom of this page.

## Switching windows

If you have several programs running at once, you can switch between them by clicking on the button on the Taskbar that represents the program you require.

It doesn't matter if you can't see a program's window. One click of its button will bring a window to the top of a pile of open windows, ready to use. This works for any program that is running, even if its window has been minimized.

## Active windows
When there are several windows open on your desktop at once, the window that you are using is called an active window. It sits on top of all the other windows.

When a window is active, its button on the Taskbar looks different from the other buttons. It looks as though it has been pressed down. An active window usually has a different coloured Title bar from the other windows.

*An active window sits on top of the other windows.*

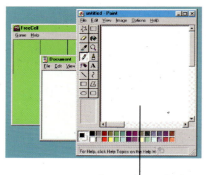

**An active window**

## Tidying up

If you have several windows open on your desktop, it can look messy.

To tidy up any open windows, click on a blank part of the Taskbar with the right mouse button. From the menu that appears, choose *C*ascade. This arranges the windows so that they overlap one another neatly.

You can arrange windows side by side by choosing *Tile Horizontally* or *Tile Vertically*.

*Cascaded windows*

*Windows tiled vertically*

## Closing
If you have finished using a program, you can close it down by clicking on its button on the Taskbar with the right mouse button. From the menu that appears, select *C*lose.

*The Taskbar*   *A program button*

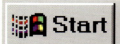  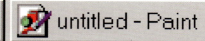

## Moving the Taskbar

The Taskbar is normally positioned along the bottom edge of your screen. However, you can move it so that it stretches along the top, left or right edge. To do this, point at a blank part of the Taskbar and, holding down the left mouse button, drag the Taskbar to a new location. When you release the mouse button, the Taskbar will cling to that edge of the screen.

## Resizing the Taskbar

Sometimes, when you have lots of program windows open on your desktop, the Taskbar may become overcrowded. You can make room for the buttons and icons by making the Taskbar bigger.

To resize the Taskbar, move your pointer over its border. The pointer changes to a double-headed arrow. You can now drag the border until you have created enough space on the Taskbar. (You can only fill up to half of the screen with the Taskbar.)

## Taskbar on top

The Taskbar is a very useful tool, so it's a good idea to make sure it is never covered up by the windows on your desktop.

To make sure the Taskbar always appears on top of everything else on your desktop, click on a blank part of the Taskbar with the right mouse button and select *Properties* from the menu that appears. In the *Taskbar Properties* dialog box, select the *Taskbar Options* tab. Switch on the *Always on top* option by clicking on it. A tick will appear in the box beside it.

When an option is switched on, a tick appears in its check box.

## Hiding the Taskbar

When your desktop becomes crowded, you can make some extra space by hiding the Taskbar. To do this, select the *Auto hide* option on the *Taskbar Options* property sheet. This makes the Taskbar disappear when it is not in use. It reappears when you use the pointer to touch the edge of the desktop where you left it.

## Missing Taskbar?

If you can't find the Taskbar, hold down the Ctrl key and press Esc. It will reappear straight away.

## Multitasking

Multitasking is a word used to describe what happens when a computer allows you to do more than one job, or task, at the same time.

Windows 95 has improved the way a computer uses its time. In previous versions of Windows, certain programs would sometimes prevent you from doing other things. Now it is much easier to do several things at once.

Multitasking is particularly useful when a computer is doing a job that takes a long time to complete, for example copying files or printing out documents. It means that you can do something else, such as writing a letter using *WordPad*, or playing a game, while the computer carries on with the job.

 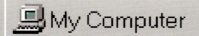 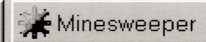

115

# Files and folders

Whenever you save a document, such as a letter or a picture, it is stored as a file. Windows 95 has two programs, called *My Computer* and *Explorer*, which allow you to see what files you have stored on your computer.

## What's on *My Computer*?

To see what is stored on your C drive, double-click on its icon. The window changes to display the C drive's contents. It contains two different types of icons, one representing files, and the other representing files grouped together in folders.

*The contents of the C drive*

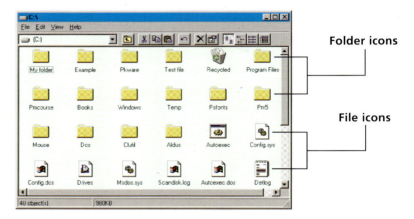

## My Computer

Launch *My Computer* by double-clicking on its icon on the desktop.

To make your display look similar to the one used on this page, check that the *Large Icons* option is selected on the *View* menu. Then, select *Options* from the *View* menu. In the *Options* dialog box, click on the *Folder* tab. Make sure the second option, shown below, is selected.

*Choose this option to view the information in a single window.*

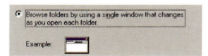

The *My Computer* window contains an icon for each of your disk drives. It may also have an icon for the *Control Panel* and your printer.

*The* **My Computer** *window*

## Folders

As you create more and more files, you should group them together so that they are easy to find. You can group files together in folders. For example, you could have one folder for work and another for home activities.

You can also have folders within folders. Any folder which is contained within another folder is called a sub-folder. For example, your home folder might have a sub-folder for letters.

## Opening folders

To open a folder, double-click on its icon. For example, try opening the Windows folder on the C drive. The *My Computer* window will change to show its contents.

You can close a folder by clicking on the Up One Level button. This displays the contents of the previous folder or disk drive.

*Up One Level button*

## Opening a file

You can open a file from the *My Computer* window by double-clicking on its icon. For example, try opening the file called WordPad Invitation that you created on page 107. It is stored in the Windows folder.

## Explorer

The *Explorer* program offers an alternative way of looking at the information you viewed using *My Computer*. (*Explorer* replaces the Windows 3.1 program called *File Manager*.) Launch the *Explorer* program by clicking on its name on the *Programs* menu.

To make your display look similar to the one used on this page, open the *View* menu and check that the *Small Icons* option is selected. This reduces the size of the icons so that they can easily fit in the *Explorer* window.

## Trees and branches

The *Explorer* window is divided into two parts. On the left-hand side, there are icons for your disk drives and some of the items on your desktop. These are displayed in a diagram that looks a bit like a tree, with lines like branches coming off a main trunk.

*The* **Explorer** *window*

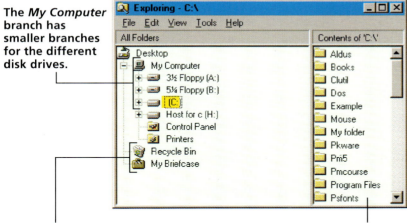

The *My Computer* branch has smaller branches for the different disk drives.

There are branches for some of the items on your desktop.

This side of the window shows the contents of the disk drive or folder highlighted on the left.

## Exploring

To open a particular folder in *Explorer*, click on its name in the left-hand side of the window. For example, try opening the Windows folder. The folder icon changes to an open folder and its contents are displayed in the right-hand section of the window.

## Branching out

A plus sign next to a folder tells you that it contains sub-folders. To see the sub-folders displayed as branches on the tree, click on the plus sign. It changes to a minus sign and a new set of branches is shown. Click on the minus sign to close the folder again.

If a folder doesn't have a plus or minus sign next to it, this means that it doesn't contain any sub-folders.

The diagram below shows a folder called Example on a branch off the C drive branch. Inside this folder are sub-folders named Home and Work. The Home folder branch has branches, representing sub-folders, for different kinds of home activities.

*A section of the* **Explorer** *window*

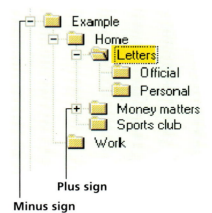

Plus sign
Minus sign

## Opening a file

To open a file from the *Explorer* program, simply double-click on its icon in the right-hand side of the window. Try opening WordPad Invitation.

117

# Organizing your files

Create your own folders for storing any files you want to keep. It is easy to reorganize your files by moving and copying them using the *Explorer* program.

## Creating a folder

Before you create a folder, you need to tell your computer where to put it. To do this, select the disk drive where you want the folder to be stored.

Try creating a folder on the C drive. Launch the *Explorer* program and click on the C drive icon on the tree diagram. Select *New* on the *File* menu and click on *Folder* on the menu that opens. A new folder will appear in the right-hand side of the window.

Beside the folder is a box with the words New Folder highlighted. When you type a name for the folder, it will appear in this box. For example, type the name **My Folder** and press the Return key. The folder will appear in the folder tree on the left.

 **New Folder icon**

## Folders in folders

You can create sub-folders within a folder using the same method. Instead of selecting the C drive as you did above, select the folder in which you want the sub-folder to appear.

## Moving a file

You can reorganize your files by moving them from one folder to another. To move a file, you simply drag its icon.

Try moving WordPad Invitation from the Windows folder to My Folder. First, find WordPad Invitation. It is stored in the Windows folder on your C drive.

You need to be able to see the destination to which you want to drag the file. Check that you can see My Folder in the left-hand side of the window. If you can't, use the scroll bar to look down the list of files and folders.

Drag WordPad Invitation's icon over the My Folder icon in the left-hand side of the window and drop it. The file has now been moved to My Folder.

*Moving a file between folders*

## Copying a file

Sometimes you may want to copy a file, for example if you want to make changes to a file but still keep the original copy.

Try making a second copy of WordPad Invitation in the Windows folder from which you have just moved it. To do this,  click on the file's name with the right mouse button and click on *Copy* from the menu that appears. Now click on the Windows folder's icon with the right mouse button. From the menu that appears, click on *Paste* to copy the file into the Windows folder.

## No entry

If you see this symbol when you drag an icon, it means that you can't drop the icon at that location.

**No Entry symbol**

## Copying onto a floppy disk

To copy a file onto a floppy disk, you use the same drag and drop technique that you used to move a file.

Try copying WordPad Invitation onto a floppy disk. To do this, find WordPad Invitation's icon in My Folder. Then make sure you can see the icon for your floppy disk drive in the left-hand side of the window. Now drag the file's icon over the floppy disk drive's icon and drop it.

If there is no disk in the disk drive, your computer will display a message telling you to insert one. When you have inserted a floppy disk, your computer will copy the file.

*As a file is copied, you will see a picture of it flying between two folders.*

## A new name

When you reorganize your files and folders, you may want to change their names. For example, when you have copied a file, you can give the second copy a different name so that you don't get the two confused.

Try changing the name of the copy of WordPad Invitation in the Windows folder. Find the icon of the file you want to rename and click on it with the right mouse button. Select *Rename* from the menu that appears. A box will appear around the name. Type **WordPad Copy** and press the Return key. The new name will replace the old one.

 **Warning!**

Only rename files and folders that you have created yourself. Renaming certain special Windows' files and folders could stop a program from working.

## *My Computer*

You can also use the *My Computer* program to create folders and to move or copy files between folders.

When creating a new folder, you need to tell your computer where to store it by clicking on a disk drive or folder icon. Then, in the same way as in the *Explorer* program, select *New* from the *File* menu and click on *Folder*. Type the name of the folder and then press the Return key.

To move a file or folder, click on its icon with the right mouse button. From the menu that appears, select *Cut* (or if you want to copy the item, select *Copy*). Click on the folder to which you want to move the item with the right mouse button and select *Paste* from the menu that appears. This moves (or copies) the file or folder to its new location.

# Finding and deleting files

However well organized your filing system is, you may occasionally forget where you have put a file. Windows 95 has a program called *Find* to help you locate any lost files. To avoid cluttering up your hard disk, you should delete any files that you no longer need. You can do this using the *Explorer* and *My Computer* programs or by using a program called *Recycle Bin*.

## Finding files

If you forget where you have stored a file, the *Find* program can help you to locate it again. Select *Find* from the Start menu and click on *Files or Folders* on the menu that opens.

**Find** icon

In the *Find* window, select the *Name & Location* tab. Enter the name of the file you are looking for in the *Named* box. Use the *Look in* drop-down list to tell your computer which disk drive to search. Click on the *Find Now* button to start the search. The names and locations of any matching files will be displayed in the box at the bottom of the window.

*The* **Find** *window*

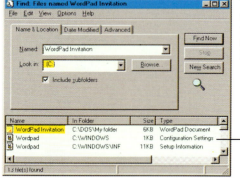

**The names of files found are displayed here.**

## Forgotten a file's name?

If you don't know the name of the file you are looking for, but you know that the document contains a particular word, select the *Advanced* tab in the *Find* window. Enter the word in the *Containing text* box and select the type of file you are searching for from the *Of type* box. Then start the search as described above.

## Deleting a file

You can delete a file using the *Explorer* or *My Computer* programs. Remind yourself how to use these programs on pages 116 and 117.

In *Explorer*, try deleting WordPad Copy from the Windows folder. In the left-hand side of the *Explorer* window, double-click on the C drive icon. Open the Windows folder and select WordPad Copy's icon. Then, select *Delete* from the *File* menu, or press the Delete key on your keyboard.

A dialog box may appear, asking you to confirm that you really want to delete the file. Check that the box contains the name and details of the file you want to delete. If it is correct, click on the *Yes* button.

You can delete whole folders using the same method. Be careful, though, because deleting a folder deletes all its contents.

## *Recycle Bin*

Another way of getting rid of files is simply to throw them into the *Recycle Bin*. You'll find its icon on your desktop.

To use the *Recycle Bin*, you need to be able to see its icon. If you have any windows open on your desktop, you may need to minimize them, or drag them out of the way.

In *Explorer* or *My Computer*, click on the file you want to get rid of. Holding down the left mouse button, drag the file's icon over the *Recycle Bin* icon and drop it. The file icon will then disappear.

When you have thrown something into the *Recycle Bin*, its icon changes from an empty bin to a full one.

**Recycle Bin** *icons*

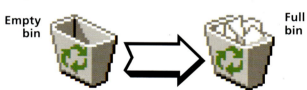

**Empty bin**  **Full bin**

120

## Whoops!

If you accidentally delete something important, don't panic! Any files that you delete from your computer's hard disk are kept in the *Recycle Bin* for a while, which means that it's possible to get them back again.

To retrieve a file, double-click on the *Recycle Bin* icon. A list of deleted files will appear. Select the name of any file you want to retrieve and then select *Restore* from the *File* menu. The file will be transferred from the bin back to its original location. Alternatively, you can drag the file to a folder in the *Explorer* or *My Computer* window.

Unfortunately, this doesn't work for floppy disks. If you delete a file from a floppy disk, it's gone for good.

## Warning!

The *Recycle Bin* doesn't keep your files forever. Normally, Windows 95 starts to get rid of the oldest files for good when the deleted files take up more than 10% of your computer's hard disk.

## Emptying the *Recycle Bin*

When you have dropped your files into the *Recycle Bin*, they still take up space on your hard disk. You can make more space by deleting the files once and for all. To do this, click on the *Recycle Bin* with the right mouse button and select *Empty Recycle Bin*. When the computer asks if you are sure, click on the *Yes* button. This will delete all the files in the *Recycle Bin* from the hard disk.

## Grabbing groups

In *Explorer* and *My Computer*, you can select several files at once by holding down the Ctrl key and clicking on the files you want to select.

*These highlighted files have been selected using the Ctrl key.*

To select a group of files, click on the first file you want to grab and then press the Shift key while you click on the last file.

*These files have been selected using the Shift key.*

You can also use the mouse to grab a group of files. Position the pointer at one corner of the group of files you want to grab. Holding down the left mouse button, drag the mouse across until all the files you want are selected.

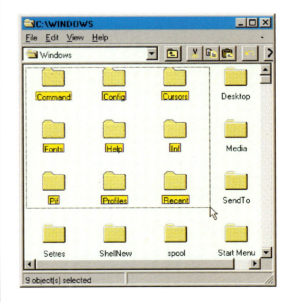

*These highlighted folders have been selected using the click and drag method.*

# The personal touch

There are lots of changes you can make to Windows 95 to give it a more personal feel. In this section, you can find out how to change the colours and patterns used on your display. You can use passwords to help you customize Windows 95.

## Making changes

You can make changes to Windows 95 using *Control Panel*. This is found in the *Settings* program group on the Start menu. *Control Panel* contains icons for the different aspects of your computer, such as the keyboard and mouse, that you can change.

You can change the way Windows 95 looks using the *Display Properties* box. Open this by double-clicking on the *Display* icon in the *Control Panel* window.

*Display* icon

Find out about some of the practical changes you can make to the way Windows 95 works on page 134.

### Take a shortcut

You can take a shortcut to the *Display Properties* box by clicking on a blank area of the desktop with the right mouse button and selecting *Properties* from the menu that appears.

## Colour scheme

You can change the colours used for the desktop and for window parts such as the Title and Menu bars. You can choose from entire colour and design schemes, or create your own.

Select the *Appearance* tab in the *Display Properties* box. To choose an entire scheme, select a name from the *Scheme* list. The example display shows what the changes will look like.

To choose your own colours, select the part of the display you want to change from the *Item* list. Then choose a colour from the *Color* drop-down list. Click on *OK* when you have made your choices.

**The** Appearance **property sheet in the** Display Properties **box**

**This example display shows how your choices will look.**

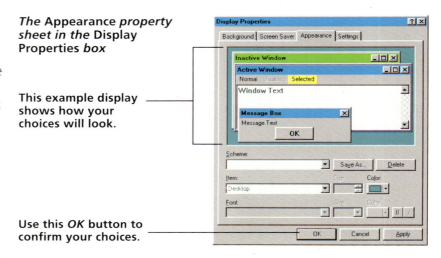

**Use this** OK **button to confirm your choices.**

## Wallpaper

Brighten up your desktop by adding a patterned layer called wallpaper to it. Windows 95 has a selection of wallpaper designs to choose from. To look at them, select the *Background* tab in the *Display Properties* box. Click on a name from the *Wallpaper* list to see a design on the example screen.

Select *Tile* to make the wallpaper fill the desktop or *Center* to display just a square of wallpaper in the middle of the desktop.

When you have chosen the wallpaper you like, click on the *Apply* button and then click on *OK*. This puts the wallpaper on your desktop.

**Clouds**

**Forest**

***Wallpaper designs***

122

## Screen savers

When you leave the same image on the screen for a long time, it can damage the screen by causing "screen burn". This means that the image is permanently imprinted on the screen.

Screen savers are programs which protect your screen by replacing the image with a moving picture after a certain amount of time.

## Choosing a screen saver

Windows 95 provides a selection of screen savers from which you can choose. To have a look at the available screen savers, select the *Screen Saver* tab in the *Display Properties* box.

Open the drop-down list of screen savers and select one of them. A demonstration of what the screen saver looks like will appear on the example monitor. When you have chosen the one you want, click on the *OK* button.

*An example monitor showing a screen saver called Flying Windows*

## Starting and stopping

When you have selected a screen saver, your computer will automatically start it if you haven't touched your keyboard or mouse for a certain amount of time.

You can alter the length of time your computer waits by changing the time in the *Wait* box at the bottom right of the *Screen Saver* box.

Once a screen saver has started, it will continue until you move your mouse or press a key on your keyboard.

## About passwords

Sometimes, a computer is used by more than one person. Each person may want to customize Windows 95 in a different way.

If you share a computer, you can ensure that your chosen colours, patterns and other changes are switched on every time you use it by creating a password system.

## Individual passwords

To create a password system, double-click on the *Passwords* icon in the *Control Panel*. This opens the *Passwords Properties* box. Click on the *User Profiles* tab and select the option *Users can customize their preferences...* Then click on *OK*.

*Passwords icon*

A box will appear asking whether you want to restart your computer. Click on the *Yes* button. When it has restarted, a box like the one below will appear. Enter your first name in the *User name* box. Then click in the *Password* box. Think of a password that you can easily remember and enter it here. Click on *OK*. A second box will appear, asking you to confirm the password you entered. Type the same password in the *Confirm new password* box and then click on *OK*.

**These password boxes appear when you restart Windows 95.**

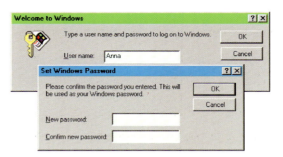

When you have entered these details, a *Windows Networking* box will appear. Click on the *Yes* button to save your individual changes for future use.

Each time you start Windows 95, a password box will appear. When you enter your user name and password, any changes you have made will be activated.

123

# Windows workshop

Windows 95 comes with a collection of programs that can help you to look after your computer. On these pages, you can find out how to use these programs. You'll also find out some ways of avoiding problems with your computer.

## Spare copies
It's a good idea to keep spare copies of all your files, called backups, in case the original files get damaged or accidentally lost. The simplest way of doing this is by using the *Explorer* program to copy files onto floppy disks. You can remind yourself how to do this on page 119.

## Multiple backups
If you have lots of files to back up, it is quicker to use a program called *Microsoft Backup*. *Microsoft Backup* is usually found on the *System Tools* menu in the *Accessories* program group. Launch it by clicking on its name.

In the *Microsoft Backup* window, select the *Backup* tab. It shows a similar structure to the one used in the *Explorer* window (see page 117). To look at the contents of a disk drive or folder, double-click on its icon.

*The* **Microsoft Backup** *window*

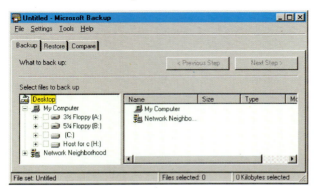

You can select which files or folders you want to back up by clicking on the check boxes to the left of their names. When you have selected the files, click on the *Next Step* button to choose where to store the backup.

Select the device to which you want to copy the files. You can use a floppy disk drive, but if you regularly back up lots of files, you might want to buy a device called a tape backup unit.

Click on *Start Backup*. The *Backup Set Label* box shown below will appear. Enter a name for the backup and click on *OK*. When the backup has been created, a message saying that the operation is complete will be displayed.

*The* **Backup Set Label** *dialog box*

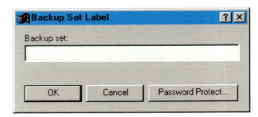

## Restoring backups
If you lose or damage any files, you can get them back again, or restore them, from the backup you made. To do this, click on the *Restore* tab in the *Microsoft Backup* window. Insert the floppy disk or tape containing the backup. In the left side of the window, click on the icon for the disk or tape drive you are using. The backup's name will appear in the right side of the window. Click on it and then click on the *Next Step* button.

The window changes to show the contents of the backup. Click on the check boxes beside any files you want to restore and then click on the *Start Restore* button. The files will be returned to their original locations on your hard disk.

### Warning!
You should make backup copies of all the files you have created before using any of the programs on page 125.

## Checking for damage

After a long period of time, parts of your computer's hard disk may wear out or become damaged. Windows 95 has a program called *ScanDisk* which you can use to check for any damage to the disk itself, or for any problems with the way your files are organized.

Launch *ScanDisk* from the *System Tools* menu in the *Accessories* program group. A window like the one below will appear. It contains a list of the disk drives that you can check for errors. Select the C drive.

There are two different kinds of check you can make: the *Standard* test and the *Thorough* test. The *Standard* test checks your files and folders. If you turn off your computer without closing down files properly, this can leave useless bits of files on your hard disk. When you run this test, it will clear these bits away.

The *Thorough* test scans the surface of the disk for errors. If there are any damaged areas, it tells Windows 95 not to use those areas when saving information or adding programs.

Select the test you want to use and then click on the *Start* button to set it going.

**The ScanDisk *window***

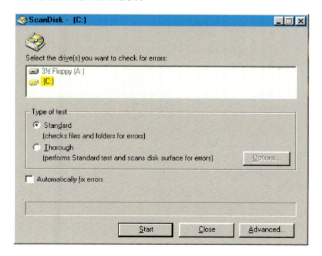

## Hard disk order

When you store files on your hard disk, they are slotted in anywhere there is space. This can cause your hard disk to become disorganized. When this happens, it may take the computer longer to find things.

You can use a program called *Disk Defragmenter* to tidy up your hard disk. This gathers all the bits of each file together so that they can easily be found. You should use it once every three or four months to keep your hard disk in good order.

*Disk Defragmenter* is usually found on the *System Tools* menu in the *Accessories* program group. Click on its name to launch it. In the box that appears, select the C drive. A box like the one below will appear, telling you whether or not it needs defragmenting. If it does, click on *Start* to set it going. If not, click on *Exit*.

**This box tells you whether to defragment the disk.**

## Shutting down Windows 95

When you have finished using your computer, you should instruct it to shut down Windows 95 before you turn it off. Switching off without doing this can damage your programs and files.

To shut down Windows 95 properly, select *Shut Down* from the Start menu. In the dialog box that appears select *Shut down the computer?* and click on the *Yes* button. If you have any document files open, you will be asked whether you want to save them.

Wait until a message appears saying that you can turn off your computer safely, then switch it off at the power button. There may be a separate switch to turn off your monitor.

# Games and gadgets

The *Accessories* program group contains lots of useful programs. Here are some of the ones you haven't come across elsewhere in the book. You can also find out how to add any Windows 95 programs that aren't available on your computer.

## Character Map

There are all kinds of arrows, mathematical symbols and other characters that you can use in Windows 95, but which don't appear on your keyboard. Use a program called *Character Map* to view all these different characters.

In the *Character Map* window, select a font from the drop-down list. The grid, or map, below it displays the characters available in that font. You can copy any of these characters to use in a document. To do this, select the character you want to copy by clicking on it. Then click on the *Select* button.

**Character Map showing a font called Wingdings**

The character will appear in the *Characters to Copy* box. Repeat this process to select more characters.

When you have selected all the characters you want, click on the *Copy* button. This copies all the characters in the *Characters to Copy* box onto the Clipboard.

Open the file in which you want to insert the characters and position the cursor where you want them to appear. Select *Paste* from the *Edit* menu to add the characters to the document.

## Notepad

As well as *WordPad* (see page 104), Windows 95 has another word processing program called *Notepad*. *Notepad* is a useful program because, when you launch it, its window appears very quickly. This means that it is handy for simple documents, or for jotting down notes or a shopping list. However, you can't insert pictures into a *Notepad* document or use different fonts and text styles.

## Calculator

Windows 95 has its own handy calculator. To launch *Calculator,* click on its name on the *Accessories* menu.

The window that opens contains a picture of a calculator. To use it, click on its buttons using your mouse, or use the keys on your keyboard to enter information.

**A S*tandard* *calculator***

You can choose between a simple calculator (*Standard*) and one which can be used for more complicated calculations (*Scientific*). These options are available on the *V*iew menu.

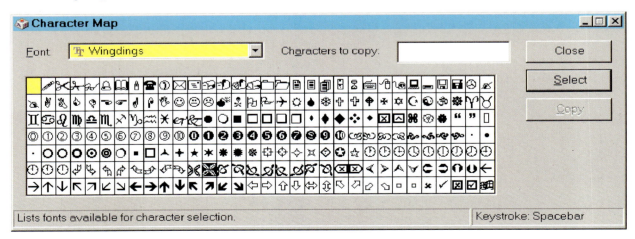

126

## Games

The Windows 95 package contains several simple games programs. They are usually grouped together on the *Games* menu, which opens from the *Accessories* menu.

You can find out how to play a game by selecting *Help Topics* from its *Help* menu (see page 136). The help topics explain the rules and give advice on how to play. To start a game, select *New* on the *Game* menu.

**Windows 95 games**

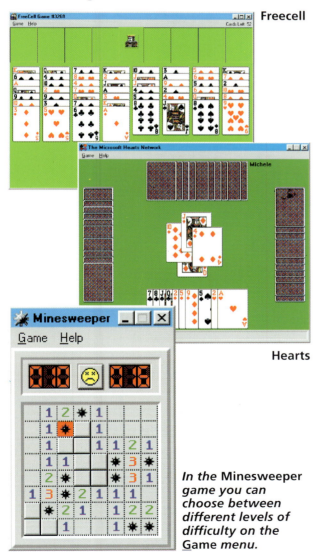

Freecell

Hearts

*In the* Minesweeper *game you can choose between different levels of difficulty on the* Game *menu.*

## Adding programs

If there are programs in this book that aren't available on your computer, you can easily add, or "install", them.

To install a program, click on the *Add/Remove Programs* icon in the *Control Panel*. Select the *Windows Setup* tab. This lists all the programs and devices, called components, that are available with Windows 95. The items with ticks beside their names are those that have already been installed on your computer.

*The* **Add/Remove Programs Properties** *box*

Certain items on the list represent program groups. When you select one of these, the *Description* box indicates how many other items it contains, and how many of these have been installed. Click on the *Details* button to see the list.

To install a component, click in the check box beside its name and click on the *Apply* button. You will then be asked to insert a CD or floppy disk with the program on it. This refers to the disks on which your Windows 95 software was supplied. Follow the instructions as they appear on your screen. You may need to restart Windows 95 before some changes will take effect.

127

# Getting connected

If you work on more than one computer, you can use a program called *My Briefcase* to transfer information between computers. You can also connect computers so that they can share equipment and exchange information. When two or more computers are connected, they form a group called a network. A program called *Network Neighborhood* can help you to work with a network.

## My Briefcase

The *My Briefcase* program offers a simple way of transferring files between computers that aren't connected. You can work on one computer and then use *My Briefcase* to "carry" your files to another computer. This can be useful if you have a computer at home and one at work or school, or if you use a laptop computer.

You will find the *My Briefcase* icon on your desktop.

***My Briefcase* icon**

## Using *My Briefcase*

To copy a file or folder into *My Briefcase*, simply drag its icon from the *Explorer* or *My Computer* window to the *My Briefcase* icon and then drop it. To transport the files, insert a floppy disk into your disk drive and click on the *My Briefcase* icon with the right mouse button. From the menu that appears, select *Send To* and then select the floppy drive. The *My Briefcase* icon will disappear from your desktop as it is moved to the floppy disk.

## *My Briefcase* update

When you use another computer, it is easiest to leave the files on floppy disk while you work on them. To do this, insert the disk and click on the floppy disk drive icon in the *Explorer* window. Then double-click on the *My Briefcase* icon. You can open a file by double-clicking on its icon. Remember to save any changes you make onto the floppy disk.

When you next use your main computer, insert the disk containing *My Briefcase*. In the *Explorer* window, click on the floppy disk drive icon and then double-click on the *My Briefcase* icon. Select *Update All* from the *Briefcase* menu. A dialog box will appear telling you which files have been changed. Click on the *Update* button to update the changed files.

**The Update My Briefcase *dialog box***

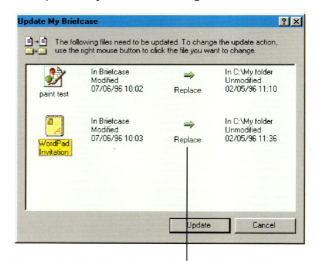

**The symbol in this column shows what will happen when you update the files. For example, here the files on the left will replace the files on the right.**

## Connecting computers

Computers in the same office can be connected using special cables. Over greater distances you can connect them using the telephone system and a device called a modem. A modem translates computer information so that it can be sent via the telephone line. This enables you to connect with computers all over the world.

128

## Network Neighborhood

If your computer is part of a network, your desktop will contain an icon for the *Network Neighborhood* program. Double-click on it to launch the program.

*Network Neighborhood* allows you to see which other computers are connected to your computer, although it only shows those computers that are switched on.

**Network Neighborhood icon**

## Workgroups

In a large network, users may be divided into groups called workgroups. A workgroup might consist of people who work in the same room or who do the same type of job. This means that files or equipment can be shared just between the members of a particular workgroup, rather than everybody on the network. Each workgroup and computer will be given a name so that it can be identified easily on the network. For example, a computer might be identified by its user's name.

In the *Network Neighborhood* window, click on the *Entire Network* icon to see a list of the workgroups on your network. Double-click on a workgroup name to see a list of the computers in that workgroup.

*The* Network Neighborhood *window*

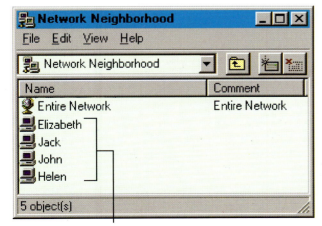

**Computers within a workgroup**

## Sharing and using

The advantage of being on a network is that you can share facilities with other network users. However, nobody on your network can use the equipment and folders on your computer until you have told it to "share" them.

## Sharing a folder

To share a folder with the other computer users on your network, find the folder you want to share in the *My Computer* window. Click on its icon with the right mouse button. From the menu that appears, click on *Sharing*.

In the dialog box that appears, select the *Sharing* tab. Then select the *Shared As* option. You can restrict what other computer users can do to a shared folder. If you choose *Read-Only*, this means that other users can only look at your folder, but can't make any changes to it. *Full* access means that other network users can change the folder. When you have told your computer to share a folder, its icon in the *My Computer* window will change to a folder being offered by a hand. You can share printers and CD drives using the same method.

**A shared folder icon**

## Opening shared folders

Once a folder has been shared, any of the network users can open the shared folder just as if it was on their own computer.

The *Network Neighborhood* window works in a similar way to the *My Computer* window (see page 116), but it allows you to explore what is on the other computers on your network as well as your own.

To see what is stored on another computer on your network, double-click on its icon. You can open shared folders in the same way. To open a document in a shared folder, double-click on its icon.

129

# The *Microsoft Network*

The *Microsoft Network* enables you to link up with other computers. You can use it to send messages and to exchange information on all kinds of subjects. It also gives you access to the Internet, a huge network which links computers all over the world.

## Joining the *Microsoft Network*

Before you can use the *Microsoft Network*, you need a modem (see page 128). You also need to join the *Microsoft Network*. There may be a free trial period of membership, but after this you will have to pay to use it. To join the *Microsoft Network*, double-click on its icon on your desktop and follow the instructions below.

**Click on *OK*.**

**Enter the telephone code for your area.**

**Click on the *Connect* button.**

**Click on each of the three icons in turn to give the information required to join. (This includes details of how you will pay.) Then click on the *Join Now* button.**

You will need to choose a Member ID and a password. Your Member ID is the name by which you would like to be known when you use the *Microsoft Network*. You enter this information in the *Sign in* box each time you connect to the *Microsoft Network*.

## Using the *Microsoft Network*

The first page that you will see on the *Microsoft Network* is *Microsoft Today*. This contains information about the latest things happening on the *Microsoft Network*. When you move your pointer over certain pictures or words on the screen, it changes to a hand pointer. This means that you can click for more information.

Close the *Microsoft Today* window. You will now see the *Microsoft Network (MSN) Central* page. This is the page you will use to start exploring the *Microsoft Network*.

**The MSN Central *page***

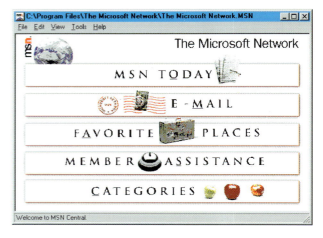

## Finding your way around

Click on *Member Assistance* on the *MSN Central* page. This contains information that will help you to find your way around the *Microsoft Network*. Try double-clicking on the *Welcome!* icon to find out how to get started.

To get back to the *MSN Central* page, click on the *Microsoft Network* icon on the Taskbar with the right mouse button and select *Go to MSN Central*. Click on *Categories* to see the kinds of subjects you can find out about. There are lots of pages, called sites, for you to look at. Double-click on the subject icons to see more information.

## About e-mail

Once you have joined the *Microsoft Network*, you can use a program called *Microsoft Exchange* to send electronic mail, or e-mail. E-mail is a quick way of communicating with people all over the world.

Before you can send a message to someone, you need to know their e-mail address. Everyone who is on the *Microsoft Network* or the Internet will have one of these. Here is an imaginary *Microsoft Network* address:
**membername@msn.com**

## Sending messages

You can launch *Microsoft Exchange* by clicking on its name on the *Programs* menu, or by selecting *e-mail* in the *MSN Central* window. In the *Microsoft Exchange* window, click on the New Message button. This opens a New Message window.

**New Message button**

Enter the e-mail address to which you want to send a message in the *To* box. Then type a short description of what the message is about in the *Subject* box. Click on the blank page area to enter your message. When you have finished, click on the *Send* button to deliver it. A message will appear at the bottom of the window to indicate that your e-mail is being sent.

**Send button**

*A* **New Message** *window*

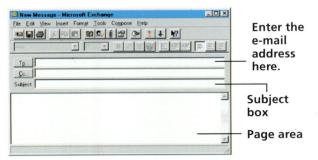

Enter the e-mail address here.

Subject box

Page area

## Reading mail

When you connect to the *Microsoft Network*, a message appears if you have received new mail. Any e-mail you receive is stored in the *Inbox* folder until you have read it.

To read a message, select *e-mail* in the *Microsoft Central* window. In the *Microsoft Exchange* window, double-click on Personal Folders in the left side of the window and then double-click on the Inbox folder. Any new mail is listed on the right side of the window. Double-click on an item to read the message.

*The* **Microsoft Exchange Inbox** *window*

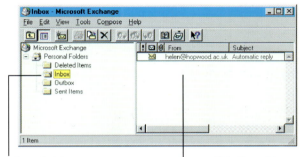

Inbox folder          Any new mail is listed here.

## The Internet

The Internet offers another way of connecting up with other computers. You can join news and discussion groups and use a facility called the World Wide Web to look up information stored on computers all over the world.

You will need a program called *Internet Explorer* to find your way around the Internet. You can get an up-to-date copy of this from the *Microsoft Network*. To do this, click on *Categories* on the *MSN Central* page. Double-click on the *Internet Centre* folder and then double-click on the *Getting on the Internet* icon. Follow the instructions provided on that page. It takes about half an hour to copy it onto your computer.

When the process is complete, an *Internet Explorer* icon will appear on your desktop. Double-click on this and follow the instructions to find out how to get started on the Internet.

# Discovering multimedia

Computers can be used to combine text, sound, pictures and video. This is called multimedia. Windows 95 has several multimedia programs. These are usually found on the *Multimedia* menu in the *Accessories* program group. Find out what equipment you need to make the most of multimedia in the Equipment box below.

## About CD-ROMs

All kinds of games and information programs use multimedia. Multimedia software is usually available on CD-ROM, a kind of disk that stores large amounts of information. You will need a device called a CD-ROM drive to play one of these.

Multimedia CD-ROMS allow you to listen to sound clips and watch video clips as well as read text. Many CD-ROMs are interactive. This means that you can click on the screen to make things happen.

*A screen from a multimedia CD-ROM*

The procedure that you need to follow in order to use CD-ROMs can vary. You will need to follow the instructions provided with each one to find out what to do.

## CD Player

You can use your CD-ROM drive to play music CDs while you work on your computer. The *CD Player* program allows you to control what's playing. It has buttons which work like those on an ordinary CD player.

To play a CD, insert it into the CD-ROM drive and launch *CD Player*. Click on the Play button to start the CD playing.

**The CD Player window**

**Play button**

## Equipment

Before you can work with sound and video you need special equipment, or "hardware". Some computers, called multimedia computers, already have everything that you will need. If you don't have one of these, you can add hardware onto your computer.

To try out the programs in this section, you will need a sound card, a fast graphics card, a CD-ROM drive, a microphone and some headphones or speakers. Ask at a good computer shop for advice on buying and adding hardware.

## Plug and Play

Windows 95 has a feature called Plug and Play. This means that it automatically checks for new hardware and arranges your computer system so that it can work properly. If you have a Plug and Play computer, this makes adding hardware very easy. When you buy hardware, you should check that it is suitable for a Plug and Play system.

*A multimedia computer*

132

## Media Player

If your computer has a sound card and a fast graphics card, you can play sound and video files using a program called *Media Player*.

If your Windows 95 software is on CD-ROM, you will have several sample files. To play one of these, launch *Media Player* and select *Open* from the *File* menu. Open the Media folder (in the Windows folder on the C drive). Select *All files* in the *Files of type* box. A list of the files will be displayed. Select one and click on *Open*.

The *Media Player* window contains buttons similar to those found on ordinary CD and tape players. Click on these to play your selected file.

**The Media Player *window***

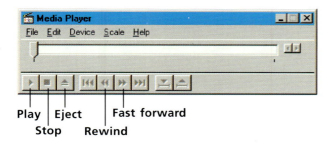

Play | Eject | Fast forward
Stop | Rewind

## Recording sounds

If you have a microphone attached to your computer, you can use *Sound Recorder* to record your own sounds. Launch *Sound Recorder* from the *Multimedia* menu.

Try recording your voice. Click on the Record button and speak into the microphone. Click on the Stop button to stop the recording. To save the file, select *Save As* from the *File* menu. Give it a name and save it in the Media folder.

**The Sound Recorder *window***

This display shows the sound waves your voice creates.
Record

## Sound effects

You can instruct your computer to play a sound when a particular thing happens in Windows 95, for example when it starts.

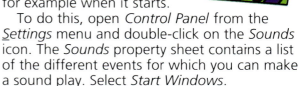

To do this, open *Control Panel* from the *Settings* menu and double-click on the *Sounds* icon. The *Sounds* property sheet contains a list of the different events for which you can make a sound play. Select *Start Windows*.

The CD-ROM version of Windows 95 has several prerecorded sounds. Select one of these from the *Name* drop-down list. To hear it, click on the Play button. Click on *OK* when you have found the sound you want to use. Your chosen sound will now play each time you start Windows 95. You can also use sounds that you have recorded yourself.

**The Sounds Properties *dialog box***

A drop-down list of available sounds | Events for which you can play a sound

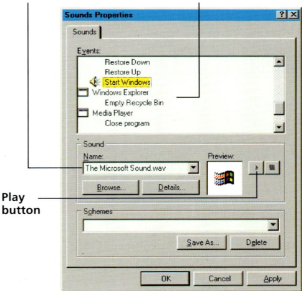

Play button

## Volume Control

You can control the volume and quality of sound produced by your computer using a program called *Volume Control*. You can launch this from the *Multimedia* menu, or by double-clicking on the Speaker icon at the end of the Taskbar.

# Tips and tricks

Here are some tips to help make Windows 95 easier to use. You can use the *Control Panel* to customize Windows 95 in lots of useful ways. You can also find out about shortcuts and other handy tricks.

## Mouse buttons

If you are left-handed, you may find the mouse awkward to use. Windows 95 allows you to change the way it works so that it suits you. To do this, open the *Control Panel* window from the *Settings* menu and double-click on the *Mouse* icon. In the *Mouse Properties* dialog box, click on the *Buttons* tab.

Choose between a left-handed and a right-handed mouse by clicking on the appropriate option button. The example mouse picture shows the effect that each button will have.

If you do alter your mouse, remember that all the instructions in this book are for a right-handed mouse arrangement.

*An example mouse shows what the buttons do.*

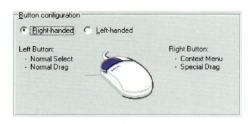

## Double-click trouble

If your computer doesn't always respond when you double-click, this may be because you are not clicking quickly enough.

To change the double-click speed, click on the *Buttons* tab in the *Mouse Properties* box. This contains a slide which you can use to adjust the speed. Slow down the double-click speed by dragging the slide to the left. This increases the amount of time that is allowed to pass between your clicks.

You can try out the new speed by double-clicking in the test area. Each time you double-click successfully, the jack-in-a-box will pop in or out of its box.

*Drag the slide to change the double-click speed.*

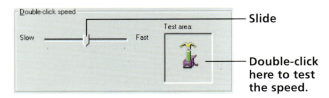

Slide

Double-click here to test the speed.

## Accessibility

Windows 95 has a feature called *Accessibility Options*. This is designed to make Windows 95 easier to use for people who have hearing or sight problems, or who have difficulty using a keyboard or mouse.

Double-click on the *Accessibility Options* icon in the *Control Panel* window to see the changes you can make. Select an option by clicking on its check box.

*The* **Accessibility Properties** *dialog box*

You can make all kinds of useful changes. For example, for people with hearing difficulties the *Sound* property sheet has options for Windows 95 to display captions or visual warnings when your computer makes a noise.

## Program shortcuts

If you use a particular program regularly, you might want to create a shortcut to it on your desktop. The easiest way of doing this is to drag the program's icon onto the desktop.

Try creating a shortcut for the game program called *Freecell*. In *Explorer*, open the Windows folder and find the *Freecell* icon. Make sure that you can see the desktop and then click on the icon with the left mouse button. Hold down the mouse button while you drag the icon onto the desktop. When you drop the icon, a small arrow and a shortcut title are added.

You can start a program from its shortcut icon by double-clicking on it.

***Freecell* shortcut**

## The StartUp folder

Windows 95 has a folder called the StartUp folder where you can put programs and files that you want to launch automatically each time you start Windows 95. For example, you could put a useful program such as *Scandisk* (see page 125) in the StartUp folder, so that it is ready to use when you start Windows 95.

To add a program to the StartUp folder, open the *Explorer* window and find the name of the program you want to add. Make sure you can see the StartUp folder in the left side of the window. It is usually stored in the *Programs* folder in the Windows folder. Then drag the program's icon over the StartUp folder and drop it. The program will now be launched each time you start Windows 95.

You can easily delete any shortcuts that you make. Simply click on the shortcut icon with the right mouse button and select *Delete* from the menu that appears.

## Clock

A clock is displayed at the end of the Taskbar. To look at the date, place your pointer over the clock. After a few seconds, a box containing the date will appear. Check that the correct time and date are shown. Your files are stamped with this information so that they are easy to find and organize. This is only useful if the information is correct.

To alter the time or date, click on the clock with the right mouse button and select *Adjust Date/Time* from the menu that appears. A dialog box like the one below will appear. Click on the *Date & Time* tab and make any corrections.

***The* Date/Time Properties *dialog box***

**Change the month in this box.**  **Click on the arrows to change the year.**

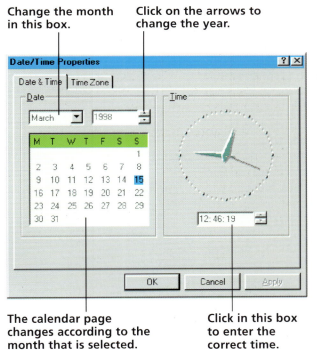

**The calendar page changes according to the month that is selected.**  **Click in this box to enter the correct time.**

## Documents folder

The *Documents* folder on the Start menu contains a list of the last 15 documents on which you worked. You can use it as a quick way of opening a document you used recently. Double-click on a document's name to open it.

There are some programs which can't add files to the *Documents* folder. If you use a file from one of these programs, its name won't appear on the *Documents* menu.

# Help!

Windows 95 has its own built-in help system. You can use it to find out how Windows 95 works, to get more information about a difficult term, or just to refresh your memory.

## Starting *Help*

To open the *Help* system, click on the Start button and then click on *Help*. The *Help Topics* window will appear on your desktop. It contains three property sheets marked *Contents*, *Index* and *Find*.

## Contents

The *Contents* section contains a general index of information organized by subject, like the contents page of a book.

Next to each item in the index is a picture of a book. Each book represents a main subject area. Double-click on a book to see more subjects within that subject area. You can close a book again by double-clicking on it.

**The Contents property sheet**

Try opening the *How To...* book by double-clicking on it and then open the *Work with Files and Folders* book. This displays a list of topics providing useful tips on using files and folders.

The topics have question marks next to them. When you double-click on one of these, a topic window with step-by-step information on that subject will be displayed.

***A topic window provides information on a specific subject area.***

## Index

The *Index* section has more topics than the *Contents* section and its subjects are arranged in alphabetical order.

To find a particular topic, type the word that you are looking for into the first box. For example, try typing **file**. The matching part of the index will appear in the box below.

Use the scroll bar to look through the list. When you see a topic you want to know more about, double-click on it to open its window.

# ⚠ Warning!

Closing a topic window takes you out of the entire *Help* system. If you want to return to the main *Help* system, click on the *Help Topics* button.

## Starting *Find*

The *Find* section enables you to carry out a more general search for help by looking for words or phrases within a topic window. This is useful if you can't find what you are looking for in the other sections.

When you click on the *Find* tab, a box like the one below may appear. This means that the computer needs to create a word list before you can use the *Find* facility. Select *Minimize Database size* and click on the *Next* button. Then click on the *Finish* button. This creates a list of all the words used in the *Help* system.

***This screen appears if you need to create a list of words.***

136

## Using *Find*

When a word list has been created, the *Find* property sheet will be displayed.

### The **Find** *property sheet*

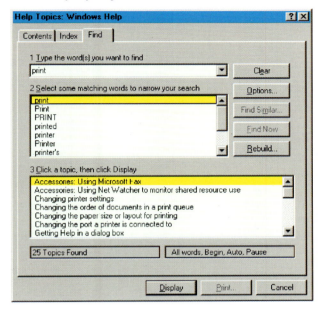

## Help gadgets

Some topic windows have gadgets to help you find your way around the *Help* system. The window below shows some of these devices.

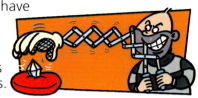

### A topic window

**Click on a button like this to take a shortcut to the box or window named.**

**Click on any word underlined with a dotted line to see an explanation of what the word means.**

**Click on a box like this to see a list of similar subjects.**

Type the word you are looking for in the first box. For example, try typing **print**. Any words in the word list that match what you have typed, for example print, printing and printer, will be displayed in the box below. If the box is blank, this means that no match has been found.

If there is a list of words in the second box, click on the one you want to know more about. For example, try clicking on **print**. A list of the topics that contain the word print will appear in the third box. Double-click on a topic to see its window.

## What's This?

Most Windows dialog boxes have a built-in *Help* facility called *What's This?*. It enables you to find out about certain features in a particular box. To use *What's This?*, click on the question mark button in the top right corner of the dialog box. The pointer will change to a pointer attached to a question mark.

To find out about an item in a dialog box, move the pointer over the item and click on it. A short description of what it does will appear. Click elsewhere in the dialog box to get rid of the explanation.

**A *What's This?* button**

### Windows 95 tour

Windows 95 has its own "tour" which gives you a hands-on guide to using Windows. To start the tour, click on the *Contents* tab in the *Help* system and double-click on *Ten minutes to using Windows*.

137

# Guide to differences

If you've used Windows before, you may find it difficult to get used to some of the differences between Windows 95 and Windows 3.1. This chart guides you through some of the main ones. You can look up a particular task and see how it was carried out in Windows 3.1 and then find out the new way of doing it in Windows 95.

| Task | Windows 3.1 | Windows 95 |
|---|---|---|
| **Program organization** | *Program Manager* gathers together all your programs in program groups. | Your program groups are shown as folders on the *Programs* menu on the Start menu (see page 100). |
| **Launching programs** | Programs are launched using *Program Manager* or *File Manager*. | You can launch a program by clicking on its name on the *Programs* menu (see page 100). |
| **Organizing files** | *File Manager* enables you to see what was on your computer and to move, copy and delete files. | *Explorer* works in a similar way to *File Manager*. You can also use *My Computer* to work with files. (See pages 116-119). |
| **Finding files** | In *File Manager,* you use the *Search* command on the *File* menu to look for missing files. | The *Find* program allows you to carry out more complicated searches (see page 120). |
| **Deleting files** | Files are deleted in *File Manager* using the Delete command or key. | Files can be deleted in *Explorer* or *My Computer* or *Recycle Bin* (see pages 120-121). *Recycle Bin* also allows you to "undelete" files. |
| **Naming files** | File names can only have eight characters. | File names can have up to 255 characters (see page 108). |
| **Switching between program windows** | You use the Alt and Tab keys or the Ctrl and Esc keys to switch between windows. | As well as using these keys, you can also use the Taskbar to switch between windows (see page 114). |
| **Making use of the desktop** | The desktop is only used for minimized program icons. | The desktop contains icons for several programs (see page 96). You can also add your own shortcut icons (see page 135). |
| **Selecting options in a dialog box** | Selected options are marked with a cross. | Selected options are marked with a tick (see page 103). |
| **Closing a window** | Windows are closed using the *Exit* command on the *File* menu or by selecting *Close* from the Control menu. | You can also close a window by clicking on its Close button (see page 101). |
| **Using programs** | You use the *Write* program to work with text and the *Paintbrush* program for drawing pictures. | The word processing program is called *WordPad* and the drawing program is called *Paint* (see pages 104-107 and 110-111). |

138

# Index

Many of the Windows words in this index apply to both Windows 3.1 and Windows 95. When a word is used in connection with Windows 95 its page number appears in *italic* type.

**Accessibility Options**, 134

**Accessories**, 38, *126-127*

active window, 12, 46, 76, *114*

aligning text, 61, *106*

address book, 78-79

Alt key, 6, 7, 9, *102*

Alt+Tab keystrokes, 9, 40

applications, 5, 37, 42-43, 51, *92, 100*

*Arrange Icons* command, 41

.BMP files, 63, 65

Backspace key, 17, *105*

backups, 124

badges, 72-73

branches
(Explorer), *117*
(File Manager), 31

buttons, 21, 46
on mouse, 10, *98-99, 134*

.CRD files, 78

**Calculator**, 38, *126*

**Calendar**, 39

*Cancel* button, 21, *103*

**Cardfile**, 39, 78-79, 82-83, 86-87, 92

cartoons, 90-91

*Cascade* command, 41, 114

**CD Player**, *132*

CD-ROMs, 22, *132*

**Character Map**, 80-81, 92, *126*

characters, 80, *105,*

*126*

check boxes, 21, 30, *103*

clicking, 10, 46, *99-100*

clip-art, 76-77, 90-91

**Clipboard**, 19, 42, 46, *105*

**Clipboard Viewer**, 19

**Clock**, 38, *135*

closing a window, 15, 25, 41, 51, *101, 114*

codes, 81

**Color**, 52-53, 92

Color Eraser, 64

colour schemes, 52-53, *122*

command buttons, *103*

compatibility, 5

Confirmation box, 30

*Contents* command (Help), 44, *136*

control menu, 25, 41, 50

control-menu box, 8, 25, 51

**Control Panel**, 52-53, 54-55, 56-57, 64-65, 83, 92, *122-123, 127, 133, 134*

copying files, 34-35, *118, 119, 124, 128*

Ctrl+Esc keystrokes, 40

Ctrl key, 6, 17, 40, *102*

*Custom Colors*, 53

customizing, *122-123, 133, 134-135,*

*Cut* command, 19, *105, 112-113*

decoding, 81

Delete key, *105*

deleting
directories, 35
files, 35, *120-121*
folders, *120-121*
text, 17, *105*

**Desktop**, 54-55, 56-57, 64-65, 92

desktop, 8-9, 40-41, 46, 50, 54-55, *96-97*

patterns, 54-55

dialog boxes, 20-21, 22, 24, 46, *103*

directories, 23, 24-25, 30-36, 51, 92
creating, 34, 51
deleting, 35
finding, 32
list of contents, 31, 32
renaming, 35
root, 23, 24, 31

directory tree, 31, 32-35, 46

directory window, 30, 31-35

disabled commands, 15, 46

*Disk Defragmenter*, 125

disk drives, 22, 58, 85, *116, 117, 124-125*

**Display**, 92, *122-123*

display, 52-53

Documents folder, *135*

double-clicking, 11, 46, *98-99, 134*

dragging, 11, 46, 99

drop-down list box, 21, *103*

editing,
objects, 29, 43, *113*
text, 18, *104-107*

e-mail, *131*

embedding an object, *113*

Esc key, 6, 7

exiting Windows, 7, 15, 125

**Explorer**, *117, 118-119, 120, 121*

**File Manager**, 30-35, 46, 51, 85

*File* menu, 22, 24, 32-33, 36

filenames, 22, *108*

files, 22, *108, 116-121, 124-125, 128*
copying, 34, 35, *118, 119, 124, 128*
deleting, 35, *120-121*

finding, 32-33, *120*

moving, 34, *118, 119*

opening, 24, 32, *116, 117*

renaming, 35, *119*

saving, 22-23, *108, 118-119, 124*

**Find**, *120*

Find section (Help*)*, *136*

finding and replacing text, *105*

floppy disk, 22, 35, 49, 58, 85, *108*

Flying Windows, 56

folders, *116-121, 129*
creating, *118, 119*
deleting, *120-121*
opening, *116, 117, 129*
renaming, *119*
sharing, *129*

folder tree, *117*

fonts, 20, 60, 80, 81, 92, *106, 126*

Format bar, *104, 106*

Format buttons, *106*

**Freecell**, *127*

function keys, 6, 7, 14

games, *127*

Glossary window, 45

greetings cards, 66-67

hard disk, 22, 58, 85, *108, 116, 125*

**Hearts**, 127

**Help** system, 44-45, 46, *136-137*

hidden messages, 84-85

highlighting text, 17, 59, 92, *104*

I-beam, 17, 46, *104*

IBM, 5

icons, 9, 12, 46, 50, 51, 96

images, *112*

inactive window, 12, 46, 76

**Inbox**, 96, *131*

139

index card, 78-79, 82, 83, 86, 87
  adding cards, 78
  editing cards, 79
**Index** section (Help), *136*
insertion point, 16, 46
installing programs, *127*
installing Windows, 5, 95
interactive story, 86-87
Internet, *131*
**Internet Explorer**, *131*

keyboard commands, 15, *102*
keyboard layout, 6

*Landscape* option, *107*
launching programs, 15, *100*
letterhead, 59, 60
lettering, 66, 70, 71
Linesize box, 62
linking an object, *113*
logos, 68-69, 73

macros, 88-91, 92
  pausing, 91
  playback, 89, 91
  recording, 88, 91
  saving, 89
  speed, 89
  stopping, 89
Marquee, 57
Maximize button, 8, 13, 50, 51, *100*
Media folder, *133*
**Media Player**, *133*
menu, 15, 46, 50, *100*, *102*
Menu bar, 8, 15, 46, 50, *100*, *102*
**Microsoft Backup**, *124*
**Microsoft Exchange**, *131*
**Microsoft Network**, *96, 130-131*
**Minesweeper**, *126*
Minimize button, 8, 12, 50, 51, *100-101*
modems, *128*
mouse, 4, 10-11, 46,

*98-99, 134*
multimedia, *132-133*
multitasking, *114-115*
**My Briefcase**, *96, 128*
**My Computer**, *96, 116, 119, 120, 121*
Mystify, 56-57

**Network Neighbor hood**, *96, 129*
networks, *128, 129, 130, 131*
*New* command, 24
newsletter, 61
**Notepad**, 37, 38, *126*
notepaper, 59

objects, 82, *112-113*
  embedding, 82-83, *113*
  linking, *113*
**Object Packager**, 82-83, 84-85, 86-87, 92
*OK* button, 11
on-line, 13, 58
*Open* command, 24
operating systems, 4, 95
option buttons, 21, *103*
*Options* menu, 30
outlined shapes, 66
outlined text, 70

page layout, *107*
**Paint**, *110-111, 112*
**Paintbrush**, 5, 9, 26-29, 42-43, 62-63, 64-65, 66-67, 68-69, 70-71, 72-73, 74-75, 76-77, 78-79, 84-85, 86-87, 88-89, 90-91, 92
Palette, 26, 62, *110*
passwords, 57, 92, 123
pasting, 19, *105, 112-113*
personal cards, 69
pixel, 28
playback, 88, 89, 92
Plug and Play, *132*
pointer, 4, 9, 46, *98*
*Print* command, 36

printers, 49, 58
printing files, 36, 58, 63, 79, *109*
**Print Manager**, *109*
p rint preview, *109*
program buttons, *101, 114*
program groups, 14-15, 50, *100*
**Program Manager**, 9, 11, 14-15, 46, 50
  closing, 7, 15
  starting program from, 15
*Programs* menu, *100*
property sheets, *103*
*Portrait* option, *107*

quiz games, 82-83

.REC files, 89
**Recorder**, 88-91, 92
recording sounds, *133*
**Recycle Bin**, *96, 120-121*
*Rename* command, 35
Restore button, 8, 12-13, *100*
Return key, 6, 7, 17, *104*
right mouse button, *99*
root directory, 23, 31
Ruler, 19, 61, *104, 107*

*Save As* command, 22, 29, 43, *108*
*Save* command, 24
saving files, 22-25, *108*, *124*
scaling, 75
**Scandisk**, *125*
screen savers, 7, 56-57, 92, *123*
scroll bars, 13, 50, 62, 66, *100, 101*
*Search* command
  in Cardfile, 39
  in File Manager, 33
  in Help, 44
selecting
  files and folders, 24, 32, 35, *121*

icons, *99*
menu options, 15, *102*
pictures, *112*
text, 17, 59, *104*
Setup box, 57, 92
sharing facilities, *129*
Shift key, 6, *102*
Shift+F5, 14, 30
shortcut keys, 90-91, 92
shortcuts,
  right mouse button, 11, *99*
  double-clicking, 11, *99*
  program, *135*
*Shrink + Grow*, 73, 77
shutting down, 7, *123*
sizing,
  an inserted picture, 42
  a window, 13, 51, *101*
software, 3, 5, 92
**Solitaire**, *137*
**Sound**, 83
**Sound Recorder**, *133*
Start button, *96, 100*
Start menu, *100*
starting Windows, 6-7, 96
StartUp folder, *135*
Status bar, *104*
stencilling, 71
stencils, 70-71
stickers, 76-77
subdirectories, 31
sub-folders, *116, 117, 118*
switching on, 6, *96*
switching windows, 9, 40, 46, *114*
**System Tools**, *124-125*

Tab key, 6, 9, 40, *107*
tab stops, *107*
tabs, *103*
Taskbar, *97, 114-115*
Task List, 40, 46
text,
  aligning, 61, *106*

140

copying, 19, *105*
finding, *105*
fonts, 20, 60, *106*, *126*
replacing, *105*
selecting, 17, *104*
size, 18, 60, *106*
styles, 18, 28, 60, 61, *106*
Text toolbar, *111*
text wrap, *104*
*Tile* command, 41, *114*
Title bar, 8, 11, 13, 46, 50, *100*
Toolbar, *104*
Toolbox, 26, 62, 66, 92, *110*
topic windows (Help), *136*, *137*
touchpad, *98*

undeleting a file, *121*
*Undo* command, 21, *104*

*View* menu
  in Calculator, 38
  in Calendar, 39
  in Cardfile, 39
  in Paintbrush, 28-29
  in Wordpad, *104*
**Volume Control**, *133*

.WAV files, 83
.WRI files, 58
wallpaper, 9, 48, 64-65, 92, *122*
Welcome box, 97
*What's this?* button, *137*
WIN command, 6

Windows 3.1
  exiting, 7, 15
  function of, 3, 4-5
  starting, 6
  versions, 3, 49
Windows 95,
  exiting, *125*
  starting, *96*
  versions, *95*
windows, 8, 46, 50-51, *100-101*, *114*
  active and inactive, 12, 76, *114*
  closing, 25, 51, *101*, *114*
  maximizing, 13, 51, *100*
  minimizing, 12, 51, *101*
  moving, 13, *101*

opening, 12, *100*
parts of, 8, 50, *100-101*
sizing, 13, 51, *101*
switching, 9, 40, *114*
Windows 95 tour, *137*
Windows 95 Upgrade, *95*
**Wordpad**, *104-107*
**Write**, 5, 16-23, 42-43, 58-61, 68, 81, 82, 84-85, 92
workgroups, *129*

Zoom commands (Paintbrush), 28, 67

Windows 3.1 and Windows 95 screen shots, icons, and box shots
are reprinted with permission from Microsoft Corporation.
Microsoft® mouse used with permission from Microsoft Corporation.
Microsoft and Microsoft Windows are registered trademarks of
Microsoft Corporation in the US and other countries.
Laptop computer (page 98) - photograph by permission of Olivetti Personal Computers.
Multimedia PC (cover and page 132) - photograph reproduced with the permission of Gateway 2000.
Usborne "Exploring Nature" CD-ROM, page 132 - Main Multimedia

First published in 1997 by Usborne Publishing Ltd,
Usborne House, 81-83 Saffron Hill London EC1N 8RT, England.
Copyright © 1997 Usborne Publishing Ltd. The name Usborne and the device are trade marks
of Usborne Publishing Ltd.
*All rights reserved*. No part of this publication may be reproduced, stored in a retrieval system
or transmitted in any form or by any means, electronic, mechanical, photocopying,
recording or otherwise, without the prior permission of the publisher.
Printed in Spain.